THE FABRIC OF

PAUL TILLICH'S

THEOLOGY

BY DAVID H. KELSEY

WIPF & STOCK · Eugene, Oregon

Wipf and Stock Publishers
199 W 8th Ave, Suite 3
Eugene, OR 97401

The Fabric of Paul Tillich's Theology
By Kelsey, David H.
Copyright©1967 by Kelsey, David H.
ISBN 13: 978-1-61097-567-4
Publication date 7/1/2011
Previously published by Yale, 1967

TO BEVERLY

PREFACE

With a host of undergraduates and seminarians of my generation, I owe a great deal to Paul Tillich even though I knew him only through his writings. He deeply shaped my religious thinking before I ever began my graduate theological education; time and again I think I have left his orbit, only to find that what I thought was my own original thinking unmistakably bore his stamp. The most appropriate response I can think of to such a powerfully imaginative theological mind is to grapple with it with all the clarity and rigor one can muster.

Since this essay takes seriously Tillich's claim to be, above all, a church theologian concerned to do theology in accord with Scripture, it is a kind of case study of one contemporary attempt to deal with the problem of the authority of Scripture for theology. The attractiveness of such a study for me personally was that it allowed me to bring together three rather diverse theological interests which I owe to several of my teachers at Yale Divinity School. I am very grateful to Professor Robert L. Calhoun, whose Socratic teaching forced me to think theologically for myself, and whose lectures in historical and systematic theology introduced me to the rich complexity of problems that need to be thought about; to Professors Julian N.

Hartt and William A. Christian who, as much by example as by instruction, showed in diverse ways how to go about philosophical reflection on theological arguments; and to Professor Paul W. Meyer in whose exegetical seminars I awoke to the challenge and theological fruitfulness of being rigorously honest with the New Testament text. More proximately, this study began in a seminar on the problem of the authority of Scripture held by Professor Claude Welch, but even more immediately, it grew out of a thorough revision of a doctoral dissertation submitted to the faculty of the Graduate School of Yale University. In that connection, to no one do I owe more than to Professor Hans W. Frei, dissertation adviser turned friend, encourager and always goad.

Much of this essay was written at Dartmouth College, Hanover, New Hampshire, while I was a member of the Department of Religion. Thanks are due the college administration for permission to use a faculty study under the eaves of Baker Library where I could write in absolute isolation (and have a magnificent view of the upper valley of the Connecticut River), and to my department chairman, Professor Fred Berthold, for congenial colleagues and the most humane of working conditions.

My wife, Beverly, typed endless pages of draft for earlier versions of this study, corrected an incredible number of spelling mistakes, and edited even more versions; for her good judgment, consolation, and sheer endurance I am deeply grateful. Although it surely is one of the more curious gifts a man ever gave his wife, this book is for her.

David H. Kelsey

Sterling Divinity Quadrangle
June 1966

CONTENTS

CONTENTS

x

NOTE ON CITATIONS

The abbreviation *ST* is used throughout for references to Tillich's

Systematic Theology (3 vols. Chicago, University of Chicago Press,

1951, 1957, 1963). The abbreviation is followed by volume and

page numbers for each citation. All exact quotations from that

work are cited parenthetically in the text; references to it, along

with citations of and references to other works by Tillich,

are given in the footnotes.

I

THE FABRIC OF THEOLOGICAL ARGUMENT

Paul Tillich stands with those theologians who hold that their task is, as Karl Barth put it, to inquire "what we ourselves must say 'on the basis of the Apostles and Prophets.' "[1] The full weight of this point is usually lost in studies treating Tillich primarily as a philosopher of religion or as a speculative metaphysician with religious interests. He certainly does have these interests, but a balanced interpretation of Tillich's theology is possible only if justice is also done to his explicit intent to be "in accord with Scripture."

The originality and boldness of Tillich's theology lies in his proposal about how to move from what "the Apostles and Prophets" said to what must be said today. One of the major ironies of the last half-century of Protestant theology is the failure to develop any consensus on this point. Ever since Karl Barth discovered "the strange new world of the Bible," a great many theologians have agreed that any Christian theology worthy of the name would be "in accord with Scripture." Moreover, they agree that theology cannot consist simply in repeating what the Apostles and Prophets said.

1. Karl Barth, *Church Dogmatics*, Vol. I, Pt. 1, trans. G. T. Thomson (Edinburgh, T & T Clark, 1936), p. 16.

Theology must state today what the Christian message has to say
to and about a world which is radically different from the world
in which Prophets and Apostles spoke. And that task, as Barth went
on to say, "cannot be taken from us, even by the knowledge of the
'Scriptural' basis which necessarily precedes it."[2] The irony is that
no precise meaning has ever been given to the relation, "on the
basis of," which is supposed to obtain between theological utterances
and Scripture. Tillich has used ontological analysis, a phenomenological account of revelations, historical research, and aesthetics to
underwrite his move from the content of Scripture to what must
be said today. In order to understand his theology fairly, it is necessary to have an accurate account of the role each of these plays.

*wt is the role in Tillich's theology of oa, pa, q, r, hr,
and a 2 argument more
for this*

The Source and Norm for Theology

Tillich has made it unmistakably plain that he regards the Bible
as providing both the sources and the norm for theology. He repeatedly states his intention to explicate "the contents of the Christian faith," or the "Christian message," or the "kerygma."[3] The
Bible "is the original document about the events on which the
Christian church is founded. . . . It contains the original witness
of those participating in the revealing events," and consequently
it must be taken as the "basic source of systematic theology." It is
his intention to write theology that conforms to a norm whose content is "the biblical message." Such a theology, he declares, would be
a theology of the church because its norm would be, not "the private
opinion of the theologian," but rather "the expression of an en-

2. Ibid.
3. Cf. *ST, 1,* 3–6, 8, 15, 29, 62.

counter of the church with the Christian message" (*ST*, *1*, 35–52).[4] First and foremost, Tillich's theology is intended to be confessional Church theology.

More precisely, theology is the explication of the "symbols used in the Christian message," because religious symbols are the characteristic form in which the content of the Christian message is expressed. Tillich has made this point quite explicit, both within and outside his *Systematic Theology:* "The subject matter of theology . . . is the symbols given by the original revelatory experiences and by the traditions based on them" (*ST*, *3*, 201). The "direct object of theology is not God; the direct object of theology is . . . religious symbols."[5] By making religious symbols in the Bible the sources for Christian theology, Tillich identifies himself with the three central themes in the reigning consensus about the authority of Scripture.

---

4. Cf. *ST*, *2*, 16.
5. Paul Tillich, "Theology and Symbolism," *Religious Symbols,* ed. F. Ernest Johnson (New York, Harper & Bros., 1955), p. 108. The following discussion relies heavily on the implications of this article, which was published four years after Tillich's *ST*, *1*. Its thesis, that the direct object of theology is religious symbols, is to be found in an earlier article, "The Problem of Theological Method," *Journal of Religion,* 27 (January 1947), which antedates the *ST*. Thus the *ST* is bracketed by substantially identical statements about the object of theology. This is important, for it puts the *ST* into a perspective that would not be so pronounced were the discussion cast simply in terms provided by the first volume, where Tillich discusses theological method. The two essays lead us to construe a great deal of Tillich's theology as an application of his thesis that theology ought to explicate religious symbols. In particular, they lead us to construe a great deal of his theology as either direct explication of one religious symbol, viz., the biblical picture of Jesus as the Christ, or as development of warrants for the way in which the picture is explicated. One would be less likely to construe Tillich's theology this way and more likely, perhaps, to take it as a discussion of ontology or of "God" or of a "saving history" if one did it solely in the light of the first volume of the *ST*.

presume here

First, what is authoritative is to be found *in* Scripture but is not to be identified *with* Scripture. The Word of God is not identical with the words of the Bible. "The Biblical message embraces more (and less) than the biblical books" (*ST, 1,* 35). Since the message is expressed in religious symbols, this means in practice that only the religious symbols in the Bible (and some cognate ones outside it) may be used to authorize what is said in theology. Everything else in Scripture is irrelevant.

Second, theology is the exposition of what Christians must say *today* to and about our world. This is the point of Tillich's concern to do "apologetic theology." It attempts to make the Christian message intelligible today by showing that it contains "answers" that correlate with "questions" implied in human existence today. "Existence" is a technical term for Tillich. It designates, not that which distinguishes real things from imaginary ones, but rather a disruption of man and his life. It is a condition of all men at all known times. It is experienced in what may be called the felt-quality of life in any particular historical epoch, and it is expressed in "questions" (*ST, 1,* 6). The Christian message must be so expressed as to show that it offers answers to the special form that these questions take in our day.

Third, what is said today must be based on what the Apostles and Prophets said to their own day. Historical-critical study of the Bible has shown that Scripture as a whole does not contain or imply any single, internally consistent, cohesive theological system. Nor can utterances found in the Bible be used as inerrant ipsissima verba of the Almighty from which, as from doctrinal "first principles," further theological judgments can be deduced. Rather, theology must result from continuing reflection on Scripture that begins ab *ab ovo ?*

ovo and takes into account all that has been learned about the history, structure, and presuppositions of biblical writings. Tillich's entire treatment of the method of correlation shows that he is fully alive to all of this. The theologian must state the existential questions to which the biblical symbols offer answers. He does this by analyzing the current "situation." "Situation" is another technical term which designates the set of ways in which men express the felt-quality of their lives. It is man's "creative interpretation of his existence" (*ST, 1,* 4). It consists not in "the psychological or sociological state in which individuals or groups live," but rather in "the economic, political and ethical *forms* in which they express their interpretation of existence" (*ST, 1,* 3–4). In the course of analyzing current culture to identify its characteristic form or style and thus discover how to frame the contemporary question, the theologian makes use of ontology and philosophical anthropology. However, this is a task of subordinate importance. The theologian does it only to the end that he may get on with his central task of giving a "methodological explanation of the contents of the Christian faith" (*ST, 1,* 28), and that is a task that can be done only on the basis of what is said in Scripture.

The symbols which are the source for theology must be subjected to a criterion or "material norm," a rule "according to which the Biblical books should be interpreted and evaluated." The Bible itself is too complex to be this norm, but the norm must derive from the Bible. The norm arises through a historical process centering in the encounter of the church with the Christian message. Consequently, there have been several different norms in the history of Christian theology, each of which arose in a different historical context. The important thing to note is that Tillich takes all such norms

The norm for present period in the NB in JATC an art UC, not the term NB in itself

to be symbols: "These symbols were the unconscious or conscious criteria for the way in which systematic theology dealt with its sources and judged the mediating experience of the theologian." The norm, or normative symbol, for the present period in theology is the New Being in Jesus as the Christ as our ultimate concern (*ST, 1,* 48–50). It is important to emphasize that this in its entirety is the norm. The quasi-ontological term "New Being" is not by itself, as some of Tillich's critics have suggested, the norm by which scriptural material is interpreted and evaluated.

This norm combines biblical symbols expressive of the Christian revelation (Jesus as the Christ) and symbols expressive of the needs of the present situation (New Being). Indeed, every norm in the history of Christian thought has combined symbols expressive of the felt-quality of life in the period in which the norm was used and symbols expressive of the event on which Christianity was founded. For example, if Tillich's analysis of the period's "cultural artifacts" is correct, the felt-quality of life at the time of the Reformation gave rise to the "question of a merciful God and the forgiveness of sins." The norm of systematic theology gave answer in terms of the symbol "justification by faith." The form of the symbol is appropriate to the form of the question. Since life's quest was expressed in terms of a question about a merciful God and the forgiveness of sins, revelation was expressed in terms of God's gracious justification of the sinner. Similarly, the felt-quality of life today, as expressed in the predominant "style" of modern culture, is the experience "of disruption, conflict, self-destruction, meaninglessness, and despair in all realms of life." It is expressed in a question about "a reality in which the self-estrangement of our existence is overcome by a reality of reconciliation and reunion" (*ST, 1,* 47–49).

JUS-
TIFI-
CA-
TION

RECON-
CILIA-
TION

question of self-estrangement answer: reconciliation and reunion

The criteria for theological answers to this question is a symbol that includes the sub-symbol "New Being." Thus, the form of the normative symbol is appropriate to the form of the question. Since life's quest is expressed in terms of a question about how to replace "estranged being" with a "New Being," revelation is to be expressed in terms of the place where "New Being" may be found.

In an article on theological method published in 1947, Tillich noted that the norm for theology today is the *picture* of Jesus as the Christ. This picture "is the criterion of all Christian theology, the criterion also of the theological use of the Bible."[6] As we shall see, this is how it must be, since the picture is all that remains today of the original Christian revelatory occurrence in which Jesus of Nazareth was received as the bringer of New Being. This picture is something actually in the Bible, though not identical with it. It is not an impressionistic image left in our imaginations after a more or less pious or romantic or hasty reading of the New Testament, but rather is in fact expressed by statements found in Scripture. The full implications of this proposal will become clear only after examining in detail what might be meant by calling the picture a religious symbol. It is clear, however, that this symbol is verbal in form and consists mainly in narratives found in the Old and New Testaments. Tillich construes this picture as an "aesthetic object" —something that is the product of the creative imagination rather than reasoned argument. It is open to the sort of critical analysis that is appropriate to objects of aesthetic pleasure, but not to the sort appropriate to reasoned arguments or to testimony offered in courts of law or to careful historical narrative. The statements constituting the picture are treated as belonging to the same logical type

6. Tillich, "The Problem of Theological Method," p. 20.

as utterances that make up novels and short stories. They cannot be taken as making any kind of fact-claim, and yet in some way they do have "content."

If this is a correct reading of the implications of Tillich's thesis that the Bible contains a picture of Jesus as the Christ which is the material norm for theology, then it suggests some of the values of his proposal. It suggests that theology is not at the mercy of historical studies that might show apparent historical claims in the Bible to be erroneous. Theology is not concerned with the Bible as historical record, but only as preserver of the picture. By the same token, theology is not subject to any claims made in Scripture about moral facts, doctrinal facts, or metaphysical facts, if such there be. The biblical picture does not *make* fact-claims; like any aesthetic object, it simply *is*. The theologian's task is to explicate what it is and to say what is to be said to and about our world on the basis of what it is.

The Structure of Systematic Theology

Tillich has repeatedly stated that theological discussion of religious symbols must not try to "translate" them or "reduce" them to nonsymbolic statements. In an essay outside the system, he suggests that symbols must be subjected to three kinds of analysis. They must be "conceptualized," a process which shows, not their conceptual content, but rather "the relation of the symbols to each other and to the whole to which they belong." The implication is that religious symbols come in sets in which they are interrelated and together constitute some kind of integral whole. They must be "explained," which "means an attempt to make understandable the *[handwritten annotations in top margin:]* conceptualized — relating symbols to ea other + to the whole 2 we ty being. explained to make understandable the relation of t symbols 2 tt 2 we ty point. CRITICIZED. Involves 3 things: ① Prevent reduction of t symbols to non-symbolic thinking, ② shows tt some symbols or more adequate tn others 2 tt encounter we xpresses its ... for symbols ③ Some symbols or inadequate in light of t totality of t symbolic

relation of the symbols used to that to which they point." They
must be "criticized," which involves three things. It prevents "the
reduction of the symbols to the level of non-symbolic thinking."
It shows "that some symbols are more nearly adequate than others
to the encounter which expresses itself in symbols" and that some
symbols are "inadequate in the light of the totality of the symbolic
meaning which they represent."[7]

We propose to take Tillich at his word and will suppose that in
his *Systematic Theology* he moves from biblical religious symbols
to contemporary theological statement by doing these three things
to the symbols. Inevitably, this involves him in making arguments;
that is, in the course of each of these three tasks he will make certain
claims and then develop a case in defense of his claims. In this study
of the fabric of his theology, our purpose will be to discover precisely what roles ontology, analysis of revelations, historical research, and aesthetics play in these arguments. If Tillich is doing
theology the way he says it should be done, one thing is clear: he
ought not to reduce biblical symbols to statements in any one of
these modes of inquiry.

Before sorting out the various roles played in theological argument by logically diverse sorts of statements, it is necessary to have
some idea of the jobs that need to be done in arguments. In this
connection it will be convenient to borrow Stephen Toulmin's proposal that arguments in general should be construed on the model
of legal arguments:

Legal utterances have many different functions. Statements of
claim, evidence of identification, testimony about events in dis-

7. Tillich, "Theology and Symbolism," pp. 111–13.

pute, interpretations of a statute or discussions of its validity, claims to exemption from the application of a law, pleas in extenuation, verdicts, sentences: all these different classes of propositions have their parts to play in the legal process, and the differences between them are in practice far from trifling.[8]

So too, any argument, including theological argument, requires different sorts of statements to fill several different functions. For our purposes it is enough to note four such functions.

1) Some statements constitute the conclusions of arguments, the claims whose merits we are trying to show. Since an argument is designed to commend its conclusion, it seems to follow that the conclusion is the sort of utterance with which someone might disagree. Here, "disagree" is used broadly to cover a variety of ways in which one might fail to accept a claim, from clear understanding but outright contradiction and rejection of the claim to vague and inarticulate unclarity about what it means. Since it is logically possible to disagree with them, the conclusions of theological arguments may be called "proposals." We shall want to learn whether the conclusions of Tillich's arguments are proposals of attitudes or proposals of patterns and policies of action or proposals for belief which alone admit of judgments about their truth or falsity.

2) Other statements assert the data adduced in support of the conclusion. We have seen that for Tillich the normative data for theological arguments are biblical religious symbols. Data "authorize" the conclusion of an argument in one way, and so in this sense the biblical symbols are the "authority" for the theological judgments

---

8. Stephen Toulmin, *The Uses of Argument* (London, Cambridge University Press, 1958), p. 96.

based on them as data. These statements need not be of the same logical type as the conclusions of an argument. In legal argument, the conclusion "Smith is guilty of murder" is a statement of a verdict of criminal guilt. It is a logically different type of statement from the statements of the data entered in support of the verdict, e.g. the reports of past events given by three reliable witnesses. So too, the conclusion of a theological argument, e.g. "Resurrection from the dead is a bodily resurrection," may be a logically different sort of statement from statements of the data adduced to support the conclusion, e.g. New Testament stories about the disciples finding an empty tomb on Easter morning and later encountering Jesus possessed of a body. What is unclear in this example is the logical status of the statements of the data. Are stories about the empty tomb to be taken as historically accurate fact-claims, or are they to be taken as having the same status as statements in parables? If the latter is true, the question of their historical accuracy is irrelevant to their functioning properly in the theological argument. Indeed, in general we shall want to know what logical status Tillich seems to suppose biblical religious symbols have.

3) Other statements function as warrants for the move from data to conclusion. Put in proper form, they are hypothetical statements which do not add to the sum of data supporting the conclusion. The distinction between data and warrants is similar to the distinction drawn in courts of law between questions of fact and questions of law. Since warrants give the rules or "inference licenses" for the move from data to conclusion, they authorize the conclusion in a different, but nonetheless authoritative, way from data. We shall want to learn whether and to what extent ontological judgments or analysis of revelatory events or doctrines in aesthetics warrant the

conclusions Tillich draws about such biblical religious symbols as the picture of Jesus as the Christ.

A final set of statements provides backing for the warrants. Backing is stated in straightforward fact-claims and is of a quite different logical type from statements of warrants. To use Toulmin's example, the warrant for the argument, "Harry was born in Bermuda, so presumably he is a British subject," is "If a man was born in Bermuda, he most likely is a British subject." The backing for this warrant, however, would be a precise statement making particular fact-claims about the terms and dates of specific Acts of Parliament and other legal provisions governing the nationality of persons born in British colonies.[9] Backing, unlike data which is also stated in fact-claims, need not be explicitly stated in an argument. It needs to be stated only when the warrant for the argument is itself challenged. When that happens, a new argument must be presented in which the original, challenged warrant is the conclusion, and its backing is the data. This, of course, requires a new warrant which might, in turn, be challenged, requiring a third argument. At some point, however, it must be possible to use a warrant that is not challenged. If such a stage is not reached, then no argument is possible at all in the field in question.[10] We shall want to know whether and to what extent ontological judgments or analysis of revelations or historical fact-claims or aesthetics provide the backing of Tillich's theological arguments.

The statements used at every point in theological argument must meet the same criteria of intelligibility that apply to statements in any other kind of argument. They cannot be nonsensical or absurd

9. This discussion depends heavily on ibid., pp. 94–145.
10. Ibid., p. 106.

or self-contradictory assertions, but they may be "paradoxical." A paradox is neither self-contradictory nor contrary to all evidence. Rather, it is an assertion "which contradicts the *doxa,* the opinion which is based on the whole of human experience, including the empirical and the rational" (*ST, 2,* 92). It contradicts received wisdom on given topics, not that which is indubitably true.

Toulmin's schema shall be used only as a heuristic device to bring into sharp relief the precise roles played by the various sorts of material Tillich has used in framing his theological arguments. Whatever weaknesses Toulmin's thesis may have as a solution for long-standing problems in logic theory do not affect its usefulness to us.[11]

Nevertheless, we must anticipate some criticism that our procedure may evoke. Toulmin's schema will help us describe the structure of Tillich's argument, the pattern in which one theological judgment is related to another. The explicit structure of Tillich's *Systematic Theology,* however, reflects the pattern in which one theological concept is related to another. Unless the distinction between the argumentative structure and the conceptual structure of his theology is kept in mind, our procedure may be criticized for imputing to Tillich's highly structured conceptual system an organizing principle wholly alien to it and thereby systematically distorting it.

Tillich divides his material into five parts. Each is internally organized according to the principle of correlation that pairs the answers found in certain religious symbols with a particular set of existential questions. Thus, Part I correlates the symbol of the

11. Cf. critiques of Toulmin in *Mind,* 73 (January 1964) and *Journal of Philosophy,* 56 (1959), 689 ff.

Logos   Truth
God   Finitude
JATC   Estrangement
Spirit   Ambiguities in morality, religion, culture

THE FABRIC OF THEOLOGICAL ARGUMENT

K T₁₄ God   Meaning of History

Logos with man's question about the possibility of indubitable and important truth; Part II correlates the symbol "God" with questions raised by man's finitude; Part III correlates "Jesus as the Christ" with questions raised by man's estrangement; Part IV correlates the "Spirit" with questions raised by ambiguities endemic in morality, religion, and culture; Part V correlates the "Kingdom of God" with questions about the meaning of history. However, the principle of correlation does not govern the way in which the five parts are themselves interrelated.

One might suppose that the sequence of five parts constitutes some sort of argument. This is suggested by the fact that, while the first part develops a doctrine of revelation and the second an ontology, Tillich considers them one in substance and uses them to develop a philosophical anthropology. One might easily suppose that Tillich thus "begins" with this anthropology and uses it to provide the criteria of truth by which he decides what else he may say about man and God or from which he infers the judgments made on other theological topics.[12]

Actually, the five parts of Tillich's theology are ordered by a quite different principle, as he makes explicitly clear. To begin with, the five parts resolve into three distinct subdivisions. The first two parts together deal with questions raised by man's essential nature, viz., that he is finite. The third deals with questions raised by man's existential nature, viz., that he is estranged from self, neighbor, and God. The last two parts together deal with questions raised by man's actual historical life. These three are not parallel, however. The first two deal respectively with two different aspects or elements

12. Cf. Alexander McKelway, *The Systematic Theology of Paul Tillich* (Richmond, John Knox Press, 1964), p. 38; cf. pp. 59–70.

of real life, which is dealt with in the third major section. "Essential as well as existential elements are always abstractions from the concrete actuality of being, namely life" (*ST*, *2*, 28).[13] Only the third major subdivision of the theology deals with questions as they are actually raised by life as it is actually lived, by life in all its complexity. The implication would seem to be that men do not in fact have questions simply about their "finitude" or simply about their estrangement, but that their complex questions raised by complex life have to be broken down into artificially separated questions for convenience.

Since the main task of Christian theology is the explication of biblical religious symbols and not the framing of existential questions, Tillich correlates sets of symbols with each of the questions discussed in the three subdivisions of his theology. He contends that the selection and exposition of these symbols is governed solely by the objective reality of God's self-disclosure in Jesus as the Christ. His intention is to construct a theological system in which Christology is central. He takes Christology to be "a function of soteriology" (*ST*, *2*, 150); that is, a discussion of that event in which there was a manifestation of a saving power. It is, then, an event in which power (for salvation) and meaning (a disclosure) are combined. The religious symbols that express the occurrence of this event in all its complexity are the symbols related to the central symbol "Spirit" (*ST*, *1*, 249; *3*, 111, 283–86). The religious symbols that express the element of power in this event are the symbols clustering about the central symbol "God." And the religious symbols that express the element of meaning in this event are the symbols clustering about the central symbol "the Christ" (*ST*, *1*, 250).

13. Cf. *ST*, *2*, 3–4.

In short, analysis of the Christian revelatory event yields the doctrine of the Trinity (*ST*, *2*, 139).[14] It is, to be sure, a somewhat unusual doctrine of the Trinity in which the Spirit has a certain priority to the other two Persons. Nevertheless, this doctrine of the Trinity is the principle according to which the symbols explicated in Tillich's theology are ordered. Once again we have the triadic pattern noted among the three questions. The three sets of symbols are not parallel. Rather, the symbols explicated in the third main subdivision of the system express the revelation in Christ in all its complexity, while the symbols explicated respectively in the other two subdivisions of the theology express two aspects of that event that have been artificially separated for convenience.

A sketch of the pattern in which the five parts of Tillich's *Systematic Theology* are interrelated does not give an outline of the steps of an over-arching argument that ties the whole system together. Instead, it gives guidance about the larger contexts in which the material discussed in each part must be understood. For example, instead of the discussion of "God" in Part II providing the basic categories in terms of which the rest of the system must be interpreted, it turns out that the discussion of "God" must itself be understood in terms of the later discussion of the "Spirit."

The fact that Tillich first develops a philosophical anthropology ought not to lead to the conclusion that he "begins" theological reflection with anthropology and therefore is logically forced to interpret all other theological judgments in terms of that anthropology.[15] A theologian does not necessarily begin his exposition with the point at which he begins his theological reflection. Tillich,

14. Cf. *ST*, *2*, 3–4.
15. Cf. McKelway, pp. 255–69.

in fact, begins theological reflection with the topic that is not treated until the last two parts of his system, the God–man relation as it is manifested in actual historical life. Since Tillich takes the normative source of information about that relation to be the divine self-manifestation in Jesus as the Christ (*ST, 2,* 95–96), he thinks that in connection with the content of theology as in all other things, he has been true to "the basic theological truth that in relation to God everything is by God" (*ST, 3,* 133). Given his understanding of Christology, his is a thoroughly Christocentric theology. It may be that there are good grounds for criticizing Tillich's Christology. He does sometimes take the event of Jesus as the Christ, not as a normative disclosure of the God–man relation, but as a "normal" example, just one instance among many, of an eternal relation between God and man constituted by a saving power that "is operating in all places" (*ST, 2,* 95–96) and not uniquely in the "Christ event."[16] One may also want to claim that there is serious distortion in Tillich's exposition of the biblical religious symbols because of the influence of his ontology,[17] but such claims need to be defended by careful analysis of the relations among the key concepts Tillich uses, and not by hasty judgments based on where he begins his exposition.

Ours is a different, if related, project. Our concern is to discover the roles played in Tillich's theological arguments by such logically

16. Cf. ibid., pp. 98–100, 174–88, for an extremely effective critique of Tillich's Christology from a Barthian perspective, and George H. Tavard, *Paul Tillich and the Christian Message* (New York, Charles Scribner's Sons, 1962), esp. pp. 52–140, for perceptive criticism from a Roman Catholic point of view.

17. Cf. Kenneth Hamilton, *The System and the Gospel* (New York, Macmillan Co., 1963), for an extended development of such a critique, made more bracing by an astringent dash of linguistic analysis.

diverse materials as ontology, phenomenology of revelatory events, historical reports, and aesthetics. These are the arguments in which Tillich moves from biblical symbol to theological conclusion and offers a case for the move. We want to know what functions as data, what as warrant, and what as backing in these arguments, and under what conditions. This sort of argumentation takes place within each of the parts of Tillich's *Systematic Theology*, but the theology as a whole does not consist of one running argument. Consequently, the structure of argument is not reflected in the structure of theological explication. Our use, then, of Toulmin's schematization of the structure of arguments ought not to be protested as the imposition of an alien form on Tillich's theology.

2

THE PICTURE, REVELATIONS,
AND SYMBOLS

The warrants for many of the things Paul Tillich says or supposes about the biblical picture of Jesus as the Christ are provided
by his analysis of the dynamics of revelatory occurrences. The
backing for these warrants consists in straightforward descriptions
of revelatory occurrences. Insofar as Scripture provides such accounts, it is a source for the backing of theological arguments. Indeed, we have already seen this at work. The judgment that the
picture of Jesus as the Christ contains the distinctively Christian
answers to man's existential questions is itself the *conclusion* of an
argument. It is an important conclusion, of course, because it tells
the theologian charged with the task of explicating the content
of revealed answers to men's existential questions where to turn
for those answers. The *datum* for this argument is the information
that the picture of Jesus as the Christ is the expression of the content of a revelatory occurrence.[1] The *warrant* authorizing the move
from this datum to the conclusion seems to be something like the
following: If a religious symbol is the expression of the occurrence
of a revelatory event, it contains that which was revealed. This is

1. Cf. *ST, 2,* 115–17.

precisely what emerges from Tillich's analysis of revelatory occurrences. As we shall see, analysis of the dynamics of revelatory occurrences provides the warrants, not only for the judgment that the picture expresses the "content" theology explicates, but also for several judgments about the nature of the picture. More generally, analysis of revelation provides the warrants for "explanation" of religious symbols.

The backing for these warrants is provided by Scripture. Tillich offers a descriptive account of revelatory occurrences which, he contends, is an accurate and adequate account of a wide variety of such events. It serves as the backing for several warrants, including the one stated above. It is intended to be a purely "phenomenological" account, free of "the interference of negative or positive prejudices and explanations" (*ST, 1,* 106). However, it is not an empirical generalization; instead, it is based on one particular revelation taken as a paradigm case, viz., revelatory event in which Jesus was received as the Christ.

Tillich defends this procedure by an argument about the nature of those events which, like revelations, occur in man's "spiritual" life. Tillich's concept of man's spiritual life is developed on the basis of a philosophical anthropology, which we shall examine later. By spiritual life he means man's active use of his "reason" to "grasp and shape reality" so that it has both meaning and moral and aesthetic value. The important point is that the products of such activity are not interchangeable exemplars of a species. One hammer may do as well as another as an illustration of empirical generalizations about hammers, but this does not hold, for example, with great paintings. "Spiritual life creates more than exemplars; it creates unique embodiments of something universal" (*ST, 1,* 107).

The basis of generalizations about any class of things produced by man's spiritual life has to be, not a numerically large collection of nearly indistinguishable items, but a paradigm instance which serves as a concrete ideal or norm to which other members of the class are analogous. Accordingly, when one tries to define the class "revelatory events," one has to choose the unique embodiment that is to be taken as the paradigm case. The instance chosen will be useful only so far as it does in fact "embody" or exemplify in an eminent way all revelatory occurrences (i.e. is "the embodiment of something *universal*"). The choice of the paradigm instance is an existential choice in that I can do nothing but choose the revelatory occurrence that has in fact been revelatory to me. The generalized account of the dynamics of revelation which is based on this one event is nonetheless an account that must fit all revelatory events. Scripture provides the only available account of the revelatory occurrence in which Jesus was received as the Christ. Consequently, it is the source of the paradigm case that the Christian theologian will use when he gives a general account of revelation. It is in this way that Scripture provides the backing for important warrants in Tillich's theological arguments.

The Function of Symbols in Revelation

According to Tillich's analysis of the dynamics of revelatory occurrences, a religious symbol may arise as the "expression" of the fact that the revelation took place, and it may also function as part of the "miracle" that occasions a second, dependent revelatory occurrence. In Tillich's view, revelatory occurrences come in families. One event is the original revelation and the others, happening repeatedly in the years since the original one, are called dependent revelations (*ST, 1,* 126). However, all revelatory occurrences, original and dependent (and both Christian and non-Christian), have the same dynamics. Each consists in a special "constellation of elements of reality in correlation with a special constellation of elements of the mind." Tillich calls the elements of reality the "giving side" of revelation or "miracle." It is genuinely objective or "other than" the self. It "grasps" the self unsolicited. In the case of original Christian revelation, the miracle is Jesus received as the Christ.

Tillich calls the elements of the mind the "receiving side" of revelation or "ecstasy."[2] In the case of Christian revelation, the ecstasy is called "faith,"[3] or, more exactly, "faith" is the name for a complex event of which ecstasy is only one element.[4] The event is the correlation of a self and a miracle. When dealt with in terms of miracle, the event is called "revelation" and is discussed as though it were totally independent of me. When described in terms of the self, the event is called "faith" and is discussed precisely as something happening to me. Furthermore, faith is explicitly identified with the state of "ultimate concern."[5]

Tillich stresses that the term "revelation" refers neither to ecstasy nor to miracle alone. Rather, it refers to those occurrences in which the two are actively interrelated "in strict interdependence" (*ST, 1,* 111). In the original revelation, the entire correlation was one that

2. Cf. *ST, 1,* 111–17, 177.
3. Paul Tillich, *Dynamics of Faith* (New York, Harper & Bros., 1958), p. 6.
4. Paul Tillich, "Reply to Interpretation and Criticism by Paul Tillich," *The Theology of Paul Tillich,* ed. C. W. Kegley and R. W. Bretall (New York, Macmillan Co., 1952), p. 338.
5. Cf. Tillich, *Dynamics of Faith,* pp. 1–4.

did not exist before. When it does occur, Tillich contends, its occurrence is expressed in religious symbols, created by those who participated in it.[6] In the case of Christianity, this happened during the lifetime of the original disciples. Tillich is content to let the New Testament anecdote about Peter's confession at Caesarea Philippi ("Thou art the Christ") stand as the symbol for this event (*ST, 2,* 97–98).[7] It does not matter how many of the details of the story are accurate or even that its factual basis may really be an occurrence that followed Jesus' crucifixion (*ST, 2,* 157). What counts is that someone at some time in some place "received" a given man (whose name perhaps was Jesus) "as the Christ." The first disciples expressed this event in their "picture of Jesus as the Christ."

Tillich attempts to show that the original Christian revelation was the final revelation in the sense of being "the decisive, fulfilling, unsurpassable revelation, that which is the criterion for all the others." The warrants for this judgment are all provided by Tillich's analysis of revelations. A final revelation is the one that contains the *telos* or "intrinsic aim" (*ST, 1,* 133–37) that analysis of revelatory events shows to be present in all of them. All revelatory events attempt to mediate truth that overcomes the conflicts between autonomy and heteronomy, between absolutism and relativism, and between formalism and emotionalism that seem to be endemic in man's intellectual life (*ST, 1,* 147–55). A final revelation does completely what all revelatory events try to do less successfully. It does it by mediating the unconditioned power of being through a finite "holy object" that does not draw any attention or loyalty to itself. Analysis of the

6. Cf. *ST, 1,* 122–23, 131; ibid., p. 41; Johnson, ed., *Religious Symbols,* pp. 108, 114.
7. Cf. *ST, 2,* 126; *1,* 107–08, 126, 133, 136.

original Christian revelatory event shows that in it Jesus functioned as precisely this sort of miracle. By his "acceptance of the cross, both during his life and at the end of it," he established "his complete transparency to the ground of being" (*ST, 1,* 133–37).

In dependent revelation, "the miracle and its original reception together form the giving side, while the receiving side changes as new individuals and groups enter the same correlation of revelation." In the case of Christian dependent revelation, the Church has been the locus "of continuous dependent revelations" (*ST, 1,* 126–27). The receiving side has been the faith of new generations of Christians. The giving side in which both the giving and the receiving sides of the original revelation are bound together is the New Testament picture of Jesus as the Christ. This picture, in all its internal complexity and mixed with a variety of other literary material in the New Testament, is all that is left of the original revelatory occurrence (*ST, 1,* 126–27).[8] Because it is expressive of the final revelatory event, the picture functions as the material norm for theological reflection by men caught up in dependent Christian revelations.

This fact about religious symbols in general, and the biblical picture in particular, is the backing for at least two warrants used in theological arguments which conclude to judgments about religious symbols. (a) If a religious symbol is the expression of the occurrence of a revelatory event, it contains that which was revealed. This, of course, is the warrant justifying the conclusion, "The picture of Jesus as the Christ contains the distinctively Christian answers to men's existential questions." (b) If a religious symbol expressive of an original revelatory event occasions a dependent revelatory event, then the same content was manifested in the two

8. Cf. *ST, 1,* 35.

revelatory events. This is the warrant that justifies the conclusion, "The primary task of Christian theology today is to explicate the biblical picture of Jesus as the Christ." To be sure, Tillich has never formulated either of these in this explicit form. Nevertheless, if his theological arguments about the nature and importance to theology of the biblical picture were laid out in candid form, these would be two very important warrants. Once this is noted, it becomes clear just how Tillich's general theory of revelation fits into the structure of his theological argument. It provides the warrants.

The fact that the biblical picture fills two quite different roles in revelatory occurrences raises important questions that will occupy a great deal of our attention in later chapters. How is the picture's role of "occasioning" dependent revelatory occurrences related to its role of expressing the original occurrence? Will analysis of what makes the symbol a good expression show why it effectively occasions revelatory events?

The Content of the Picture

The biblical picture of Jesus as the Christ is the expression of a revelatory occurrence. But what is the content that is expressed? In order to answer that, we need to note what Tillich identifies as the content that is manifested in any revelation.

According to Tillich, revelation is not a disclosure of special information which gives us new knowledge. Rather, it is a mediation of power that gives ontological "healing" or "salvation." For Tillich, revelation *is* salvation (*ST, 2,* 166–67; *1,* 146).[9] "Revela-

9. For the background in Tillich's early thought for the general theory of religion sketched here, see James Luther Adams, *Paul Tillich's Philosophy of Culture, Science, and Religion* (New York, Harper & Row, 1965), Chap. 5.

tion is a manifestation of what concerns us ultimately," and what concerns us ultimately, Tillich says, "is that which determines our being or not-being" (*ST, 1*, 110, 14). What determines our being or not-being may be called the "power of being" or the "ground of being." The power of being is "mystery" because it cannot, properly speaking, be known. It is the "Divine Spirit," or "God Present" (*ST, 3*, 107, 111). Its manifestation does not yield "information about divine things"; rather,

> it is the ecstatic manifestation of the Ground of Being in events, persons, and things. Such manifestations have shaking, transforming, and *healing power*. They are saving events in which the power of the New Being is present. (*ST, 2*, 166–67; my italics)

In dependent Christian revelation, it is the picture of Jesus as the Christ that "mediates the transforming power of the New Being" (*ST, 2*, 115). Indeed, according to Tillich, this power is the substance of the New Testament picture of Jesus as the Christ. He admits that the picture is given to us in the New Testament in a variety of forms or "frames," but "one must distinguish between the symbolic frame in which the picture of Jesus as the Christ appears and the substance in which the *power* of the New Being is present." In spite of the variety of frames, "in all cases the substance is untouched. It shines through as the *power* of the New Being" (*ST, 2*, 138; my italics). Tillich variously identifies this transforming or healing power with the "Divine Spirit," the "Spiritual Presence," the "Presence of God," "agape," and "grace."[10] For convenience, we shall continue to use "New Being." In original Christian revela-

10. Cf. *ST, 3*, 107, 111, 140, 274.

tion, Jesus himself was "the bearer of the New Being" (*ST*, *2*, 121) to his disciples. The picture of Jesus as the Christ is the way in which the disciples expressed their experience of receiving the "transforming power of the New Being" in the original revelation. It itself then becomes the giving side of dependent revelation. The picture is revelatory in the same sense that Jesus was revelatory: in their respective modes of revelation they fill the same function, viz., they mediate to us the power of the New Being.

The experience of receiving "the transforming power of the New Being" can be described phenomenologically in at least two ways. First, the experience involves an act of sudden discernment. Although Tillich does not explicitly use this term to describe this aspect of the experience, he does say that in ecstasy the intellectual act that normally leads to the drawing of a conclusion is "replaced by insight" (*ST*, *3*, 256).

Ecstasy, he says, involves both a "shock" and an experience of "elevating power." The shock is the same as the shock that is said to give rise to ontology. It is a discernment or insight into one's own ontological "threatenedness" which is "resisted" by an inexplicable power of being. When one tries to exercise reason to grasp this power and thereby assure oneself of one's ontological well-being, one finds that "reason reaches its boundary line, is thrown back upon itself, and then is driven again to its extreme situation."

When the shock gives rise to ontology, only the shock is experienced. In ecstasy, however, the shock is "overcome" by the experience of elevating power (*ST*, *1*, 113). Ecstasy has this additional side because it involves discernment into more than one's "threatenedness." It involves the additional discernment that one is in fact now related to the power of being. One may not be able to "know" the power of being itself, but one can "know" that one is in relation to it. As Tillich puts it, in revelation,

> something more is known of the mystery [i.e. the power of being] after it has become manifest in revelation. *First*, its reality has become a matter of experience. *Second*, our relation to it has become a matter of experience. Both of these are cognitive elements. But revelation does not dissolve the mystery into knowledge [i.e. into knowledge about the power of being in itself]. (*ST, 1,* 109)

These two things known ought to be taken in reverse order.

Fundamentally, in revelation one comes to be aware (as the second of the things known in revelation) that one is related to the "unconditioned" power of being. The man who has not had certainty about this receives a new certainty. One is given the felt-presence of the power of being. Ontological analysis can point out that in fact I am related to the unconditioned. On this point, ontology can lead me to say what revelation gives me to experience. But thinking through the ontological analysis cannot bring me to an immediate awareness of this relatedness; it cannot induce or evoke a sense of the felt-presence of the unconditioned. This is precisely what revelation does.

Hence, it can be said (as the first of the things known in revelation) that revelation makes the reality of the unconditioned become a "matter of experience," i.e. its reality as an effective presence in my actual life. In faith, "Man is conscious of the Spiritual Presence's work in him" (*ST, 3,* 133). It is precisely this that allows the identification of ecstasy with "ultimate concern." Ecstasy is a kind of concern in that it is a total absorption of the self in the experience of the felt-presence of the unconditioned. It is truly "ultimate concern" in the sense that it is concern with that which is truly "ultimate," viz., the unconditioned power of being. This side of ecstasy is said to be elevating because it is experienced as healing by men who previously had felt life to be self-contradictory and driving to ontological self-destruction (*ST*, *2*, 60). Since being "healed" is what is meant by being "saved" (*ST*, *2*, 166), this may equally well be called an experience of salvation. Revelation *is* salvation.

Tillich has explicitly connected the healing or elevating aspect of revelation with coming to discernment by comparing revelation with the therapeutic insight that comes in the course of psychoanalysis:

> Recently the term "insight" has been given connotations of *gnosis*, namely, of a knowledge which transforms and heals. Depth psychology attributes healing powers to insight, meaning not a detached knowledge but a repetition of one's actual experiences. . . . Insight in this sense is a reunion with one's own past. . . . Such cognitive union produces a transformation just as radical and as difficult as that presupposed and demanded by . . . Paul. (*ST*, *1*, 96)

So too in revelation one experiences by an act of insight or discernment a reunion with the power of being.[11] It is felt to be "transforming."

This discernment is "momentary." Its content is inseparable from the time and manner in which it is received. The content is a discernment about ourselves as we are in the moment of discernment.

---

11. This "discernment" is clearly an instance of what Tillich in other contexts and from the earliest period of his writings has called having "religious knowledge." Cf. Paul Tillich, *The Protestant Era* (Chicago, University of Chicago Press, 1948), p. 217.

Revelation gives "knowledge about the revelation of the mystery of being to us," viz., the therapeutic awareness that in the present moment one does, in fact, apprehend the unconditioned. We have precisely this insight, i.e. precisely a therapeutic one, only in this moment. It may be that we shall have it in another moment too, but all we know in the revelatory situation is that we are having it now. It "does not increase our knowledge about the structures of nature, history and man"; consequently, "it cannot be introduced into the context of ordinary knowledge as an addition, provided in a peculiar way, yet independent of this way once it has been received." It "can be received only in the situation of revelation, and it can be communicated—in contrast to ordinary knowledge—only to those who participate in this situation" (*ST, 1,* 129).

The second way in which the experience of receiving "the transforming power of the New Being" can be described is to say that it is an "experience of the holy." In order to specify the features of this experience, Tillich simply appropriates Rudolph Otto's phenomenology of the holy.[12] In Tillich's view, the experience of the holy has two aspects: it is an experience in which one is "ultimately concerned" and it is an experience "of unconditional power": "An analysis of this experience shows that wherever the holy appears it is a matter of ultimate concern both in attracting and repelling, and of unconditional power, both in giving and in demanding."[13]

In the experience, one is so intensely attracted and repelled, fascinated and shaken by something "mysterious,"[14] that one finds

12. Tillich, *Dynamics of Faith,* p. 13; cf. *ST, 1,* 215; *3,* 256.
13. Paul Tillich, "The Meaning and Justification of Religious Symbols," *Religious Experience and Truth,* ed. Sidney Hook (New York, New York University Press, 1961), p. 7.
14. Tillich, *Dynamics of Faith,* p. 15.

oneself ultimately concerned. Tillich correlates Otto's description of this experience (*mysterium fascinans et tremendum*) with the two aspects of the ecstasy in which one receives the manifestation of the "mystery of being." One experiences shock in the sudden awareness that one is so dependent on the unconditioned as to be threatened by it; one is shaken and repelled by the manifested mystery. This is the experience of *mysterium tremendum*. One also experiences an elevating power by which one's ontological health is preserved; one is attracted and fascinated by the manifested mystery. This is the experience of the *mysterium fascinosum* (*ST, 1,* 113). The preoccupation with that concrete thing which seems to exhibit the quality of holiness (*ST, 1,* 215) *is* the "concern" of "ultimate concern."

Precisely because it involves an experience of the holy, this experience can be called a distinctively religious experience. "The *basic* religious experience is that of the presence of the holy in concrete things, persons, or actions here and now."[15] Hence, it is fair to classify the act of discernment that is integral to this experience as a "religious discernment."

This part of Tillich's analysis of the dynamics of revelation yields the following warrant: If something is a genuine religious symbol, then, in the odd discernment and experience of the holy which we undergo in the presence of the symbol, it mediates to us a "healing" power. This may be used, among other things, to license judgments about the genuineness or validity of a religious symbol.

This raises in a new form the important question already noted. If the content of a religious symbol is the power it mediates, how is this content related to features of the symbol in virtue of which

15. Tillich, "The Meaning and Justification of Religious Symbols," p. 9.

it is expressive and intelligible? For example, in a symbol like the biblical picture which is cast in verbal terms, what is the relation between the formal features of its discourse and the fact that it mediates a healing power?

Religion or Revelation?

If revelation *is* salvation and salvation can be phenomenologically described as the joint occurrence of discernment and an encounter with the holy, then is not revelation simply another name for religious experience or at least for one sort of religious experience? And, since the picture arises in this experience, is not theology the explication of the contents of human religious experience rather than of divine self-manifestation? Tillich goes out of his way to insist that this is an erroneous conclusion. It is "wrong to identify religion with revelation" (*ST, 2,* 80). If Christianity makes an "unconditional and universal claim," it is "not based on its own superiority over other religions," for as a religion it is "neither final nor universal." It can make such claims only insofar as it "witnesses to the final revelation" (*ST, 1,* 134). Tillich is as insistent on the opposition of revelation to religion as is any "neo-reformation" theologian. Nevertheless, his treatment of the distinction between religion and revelation seems in places to be confused.

Tillich bases his defense on the point that religious experience is just one aspect of one element of a complex whole. It is experience of the holy, and it must be joined with a discernment about one's relation to the power of being before it can count as the receiving side of a revelatory occurrence. Even then, religious experience is an aspect of only one element in a larger whole, for the receiving side has to be correlated with a giving side before either can count as an element in a genuinely revelatory occurrence. And "revelation" is usually used to designate the entire occurrence in which religious experience is merely one aspect of one element.

Tillich's concern to distinguish revelation from religious experience probably rises out of a desire to avoid being construed as a "reductionist." If revelation were nothing more than religious experience, then both revelation and the experience might easily be further explained or "reduced" by being exhaustively accounted for by psychology or physiology. Revelation is something more than an honorific name for the manifestations of a personality quirk or chemical imbalance in the believer. The "something more" in revelation is the giving side of the occurrence.

The giving side is as much an act as is the receiving side: it "grasps" men (*ST, 1,* 111, 112, 117). Sometimes Tillich seems to personify the unconditioned power of being and speaks of it objectifying itself in the form of concrete symbols which are the giving sides of revelatory occurrences: "the mystery [of being] . . . expresses *itself* in symbols and myths which point to the depth of reason and its mystery" (*ST, 1,* 110; my italics). In the case of original Christian revelation this means that "the objective reality of the New Being precedes subjective participation in it" (*ST, 2,* 177). Thus, Tillich seems to argue that the person of Jesus of Nazareth, independently of his being received as the Christ, "has the quality of the New Being beyond the split of essential and existential being" (*ST, 2,* 121). The objective presence of this quality precedes its reception in a healing way by men. Hence, even though "those who have encountered him are only fragmentarily healed," nevertheless "we must say that in him," independent of our reception of him, "the healing quality is complete and unlimited" (*ST, 2,* 168).

The same thing holds for dependent Christian revelation:

> the message of conversion is, first, the message of a new reality to which one is asked to turn; in the light of it, one is to turn away from the old reality, the state of estrangement in which one has lived. (*ST, 2,* 177)

That is, the address to me by the message (i.e. the biblical picture of Jesus as the Christ) is prior to my response of receiving it. Since this message comes expressed in religious symbols, theology has the task of explicating these symbols to get at the message.

This has a very important implication for theology. Religious symbols are important to theology only insofar as they express the occurrence of the original revelatory event. *That* is what is "given" to man and can never be produced by man out of his religious experience. Theology ought not to be concerned with symbols that merely express somebody's religious experience. Such symbols would express the religious dimension of the felt-quality of life. They would, in short, be part of the "situation."[16] As we have seen, however, the situation implies not the answers, but the questions. Only revelation and the symbols expressive of the revelatory occurrence imply the answers.

Tillich seems to think of the giving side of both original and dependent Christian revelatory occurrences as somehow bursting out on a man and seizing him. This act of giving is just as much a constituent element in the complex revelatory occurrence as is a man's

16. Cf. *ST, 2,* 15.

act of receiving it. Tillich makes the same point another way by insisting that religious experience does not itself produce the giving side; reception does not create revelation:

> The event on which Christianity is based . . . is not derived from experience; it is *given* in history. Experience is not the source from which the contents of systematic theology are taken but the medium through which they are existentially received. (*ST, 1,* 42)[17]

There is something more to a revelatory occurrence than the experiential, receiving side: it is an event "given" in history.

The contention that experience can be a medium without being the source of revelation is defended by an elaborate analysis of three senses of experience. Of the three, only mystical experience can serve as the medium of revelation. This sort of experience "receives and does not produce" (*ST, 1,* 42–46). Tillich discusses this notion somewhat more clearly in an essay outside the system. There he identifies the medium of revelation with "the element of immediacy." This in turn is identified with "the awareness of the ultimate itself":

> It is wrong to call this point "God" (as the ontological argument does), but it is necessary to call it "that which makes it impossible for us to escape God." It is the presence of the element of "ultimacy" in the structure of our existence, the basis of religious experience. It has been called "religious *a priori*": but if we use this phrase . . . *we must remove every content from it* and reduce

17. Cf. *ST, 1,* 113.

it to *the pure potentiality of having experiences* with the character of "ultimate concern."[18]

The experience which is the medium for revelation turns out to be the a priori possibility in me for my participating in a revelatory-saving occurrence. In virtue of it, I can participate in revelation and be aware of it; to that extent it is the possibility of my experiencing revelation. On this basis it is possible to say: In order for a revelatory occurrence to take place it is necessary that I have religious experience in the sense that it is necessary for me to be able to participate as receiver in that occurrence. Nevertheless, the revelatory occurrence is not simply constituted by my act of having religious experience. There is something else quite independent of my act of reception, and that is the act of giving.

If this is correct, it is a mistake to claim that Tillich recognizes two sources of knowledge of God, the "religious a priori" found in all men and concrete revelations found only at particular times and places.[19] In Tillich's sense of the term, "knowledge" of God comes only in particular events. These are complex events that can be analyzed into two factors, the "pure potentiality of having experience" and a "miracle" or "holy object." Neither alone provides knowledge of God. That comes only when the a priori is met by a miracle, and by definition such an occurrence is a revelatory event. Were man not living in existential estrangement, the religious a priori would be sufficient. But in fact actual men are estranged and the only knowledge of God they may ever have comes in revelation, though, of course, not necessarily revelation in Christ.

18. Tillich, "The Problem of Theological Method," pp. 22–23 (my italics).
19. Cf. Hamilton, *The System and the Gospel*, pp. 54–74.

We noted at the start of this discussion of the relation between revelation and religious experience that Tillich uses the term "revelation" inconsistently. Usually he uses it to refer to the entire revelatory occurrence, but sometimes he uses it to refer only to the giving side of that occurrence.[20] This inconsistency leads to a serious muddle when Tillich applies his distinction between revelation and religious experience to the occurrence of the original Christian revelatory event: "The event on which Christianity is based . . . is not derived from experience; it is *given* in history" (*ST, 1,* 42). The event on which Christianity is based is revelation. History or human experience is the medium of that revelation, but it is not the source of it.

Note that the way the antithesis is stated in this passage makes revelation stand as though contrasted with religious experience by mutual exclusion. Experience might be the receiving side, but it only receives; revelation is the giving side. This is what makes revelation truly "other than" religious experience.

The disjunction between revelation and experience seems to produce two warrants to help the theologian distinguish which symbols should occupy his attention: If a religious symbol expresses the fact that a revelatory event has occurred, it expresses the giving side of the occurrence and thus expresses an extra-human act; if a religious symbol expresses a religious experience, then it expresses the receiving side of the occurrence and thus expresses a purely human act. The theologian, of course, should explicate the contents of the first kind of symbol if he wants to give an exposition of revealed answers to men's existential questions.

20. Paul Tillich, *Biblical Religion and the Search for Ultimate Reality* (Chicago, University of Chicago Press, 1955), p. 4; hereafter cited as *Biblical Religion.*

This disjunction between revelation and experience cannot be made in Tillich's terms, however. Consequently, the claim that theology is concerned with the symbols expressing the occurrence of revelation but not with the symbols expressing religious experience cannot be made either.

Tillich's entire discussion of the rise of the church and Christian faith makes it quite clear that the event on which Christianity is founded is not the merely giving side of original Christian revelation, but rather the *total* revelatory occurrence, including both of its sides. If this is so, then the event on which Christianity is based clearly is in part derived from experience; that is, one aspect of the event is the religious experience constituting the receiving side of the event.

Tillich insists that it is not Jesus of Nazareth but Jesus as the Christ who is the giving side of original revelation. To say he is Jesus as the Christ is to say that he is the one "who brings the new state of things, the New Being" (*ST, 2,* 97). However, Jesus can be said to be this only if in fact he does bring the power of New Being to somebody; that is, he can be called "the Christ" only if he is received in ecstasy: "Without this reception the Christ would not have been the Christ, namely the manifestation of the New Being in time and space" (*ST, 2,* 99). The giving side, then, is not wholly independent of the receiving side. On the contrary, its being received seems to be a necessary condition of its being the giving side of precisely revelatory occurrences. Thus, religious experience (i.e. an act of receiving) is a necessary condition for there being an event on which Christianity is based. Consequently, the flat disjunction between event given in history and event at least partly derived from experience is illicit.

Similarly, Tillich insists that it is not the biblical narratives as such but the biblical narratives received in ecstasy that serve as the giving side of dependent revelation. The Bible contains reports of miracles (i.e. the giving side of an original revelation in the past). However,

> The knowledge of such reports, and even keen understanding of them, does not make them revelatory for anyone who does not belong to the group which is grasped by the revelation. There is no [dependent] revelation if there is no one who receives it as his ultimate concern [i.e. in ecstasy]. (*ST, 1,* 111)[21]

Thus, in dependent revelatory occurrences, too, a religious experience (act of receiving) is a necessary condition for there being a giving side in a truly revelatory event. In this case also, the disjunction between event given in history and event at least in part derived from experience is illicit.

Surely Tillich cannot have it both ways. If he wants to insist that the subject matter of theology is not religious experience or the symbols in which religious experience is expressed, but rather is revelation and the symbols in which revelation is expressed, then he needs to insist on the disjunction between religious experience and revelation, between the act of receiving and the act of giving in the total revelatory occurrence. There is good reason to do this. If he does not, he runs the risk of developing a theology that is one more piece of evidence in support of Feuerbach's thesis that all talk about God is really talk about man, all talk about God's act is really talk about man's act. If Tillich does do this, however, he cannot also maintain (as he seems to try to do) that revelation is a complex

21. Cf. *ST, 1,* 117, 125, 127; *2,* 115.

event in which a human act (reception) is integral and essential. The dilemma is the more poignant because there is also good reason for insisting on this second point. If human response is not integral to the occurrence called "revelation," then one runs the risk of making the absurd claim that God has in fact made himself known without anyone necessarily knowing it!

This muddle raises the question of how one can distinguish between a religious symbol expressive of a revelatory occurrence and a symbol expressive of a religious experience. If, as seems to be the case, it is impossible to separate these two functions of religious symbols, is it possible to give an exposition of revealed answers that is not hopelessly fused with an exposition of human self-awareness? In short, is it possible to do theology Tillich's way and not end up supporting Feuerbach's dictum that theology is really anthropology? It may be that this question, as stated, is unanswerable. At least there is little evidence that any Protestant theologian has answered it adequately. Nevertheless, it is a question raised by the way Tillich himself sets up the issues, and so it is fair to ask whether he has answered it.

Revelations and Religious Symbols

Tillich's perplexing notion of religious symbols is most helpfully interpreted in the content of his analysis of revelations. Close reading of Tillich's descriptions of religious symbols shows that they have a point for point correspondence with his account of the miracle element in revelatory events. It may be that "religious symbol" is just another term for "miracle." At the very least the class "religious symbols" includes all miracles. This means that analysis of revelatory events, and especially of the way miracles function in them, provides the warrants for judgments about religious symbols.

It is important to locate Tillich's discussion of religious symbols properly within his analysis of revelations, for it also shows how he undertakes the "explanation" of religious symbols. This is the second of the three things he said theology must do to symbols. The other two are conceptualization, which we will examine in Chapter 5, and criticism, which we shall discuss in Chapter 6. But explanation must be discussed here, for it consists in the "attempt to make understandable the relation of the symbols used to that to which they point."[22] This is done, we contend, by analysis of revelatory events and not, as might be thought, by ontological analysis.

Our discussion will be based on Tillich's most recent account of religious symbols. He has formulated and reformulated his general account of symbols, as opposed to signs, in a series of articles written over thirty-five years,[23] but his critics continue to complain that it remains obscure. Since the most recent exposition originated as a paper for a colloquium of philosophers and theologians gathered

22. Johnson, ed., *Religious Symbols*, p. 111 passim.
23. Tillich's discussion of this topic began in 1928 and has continued in at least five different important essays. Each essay involves a slight modification of the immediately preceding one, and it is difficult to tell whether these verbal changes indicate changes in theory. This perplexity is made more acute by the fact that Tillich has continued to have his earliest essay republished (in 1940, 1958, 1961), most recently as an "appendix" to the work in which the newest version of his position is published. Whether this juxtaposition is intended to emphasize the shift in his views or to suggest that the newer statement is simply a commentary on the earlier is unclear. I believe that in his effort to clarify his position Tillich has changed it at some points. In an uncertain and faltering kind of way he seems to be moving from an explication of "symbols" in terms of his "ontology" to an explication of them in terms of their function in religious life. At any rate, the five essays are "The Religious Symbol," trans. James Luther Adams, with the assistance of Ernst Fraenkel, *Journal of Liberal Religion*, 2 (1940), 13–33 (This first appeared in *Blaetter fuer deutsche Philosophie* [Ed. 1, H. 4, 1928] and then was reprinted in *Religioese Verwirklichung* [Berlin, 1930]. It is reprinted in *Daedalus*, Summer 1958 [*Proceedings of the*

expressly to discuss this topic, we may suppose that in it Tillich has done his best to satisfy his critics.[24]

In this discussion Tillich distinguishes "representative symbols" from "discursive symbols" and locates "religious symbols" as a subset of the first group. Representative symbols as a class are found in language, history, the arts, and religion and have the following characteristics:

they point beyond themselves to that which they symbolize;

they participate in the reality of that which they represent;

they cannot be created at will because they depend on a social matrix;

they open up "dimensions of reality" in correlation to "dimensions of the human spirit";

they have an "integrative and disintegrative" power over individuals and groups.[25]

American Academy of Arts and Sciences, 87], pp. 3–21 and as an "appendix" to *Religious Experience and Truth*, ed. Hook, pp. 301–21); "God as Being and the Knowledge of God," *ST, 1,* 238–41; "The Nature of Religious Language," *Christian Scholar, 38* (September 1955) (This was reprinted in *Theology of Culture*, ed. Robert C. Kimball [New York, Oxford University Press, 1959], pp. 53–68); "Existential Analyses and Religious Symbols," *Contemporary Problems in Religion*, ed. H. A. Basilius (Detroit, Wayne University Press, 1956), pp. 35–57 (This was reprinted in *Four Existentialist Theologians*, ed. Will Herberg [Garden City, Doubleday Anchor Books, 1958], pp. 41–55); "The Meaning and Justification of Religious Symbols," *Religious Experience and Truth*, ed. Hook, pp. 3–12.

24. The fourth annual New York University Institute of Philosophy met in New York, October 21–22, 1960.

25. Tillich, "The Meaning and Justification of Religious Symbols," pp. 3–6.

We can see from the very first item that to explain what religious symbols are is to engage in theology's task of explanation.

Religious symbols differ from other representative symbols because they alone "mediate ultimate reality through things, persons, and events." How can we tell when a symbol is in fact mediating "ultimate reality"? One might expect the answer to be given in terms of an ontological analysis demonstrating the existence of "ultimate reality" and describing its characteristics so that we can recognize it when symbols mediate it. Indeed, Tillich himself says that ontology is one way to specify the referent of religious symbolism, but he makes it clear that ontological analysis can never give a description of that referent. All it can describe are the most general features of finite reality. Consequently, ontology does not provide independent information about the referent of religious symbols by which one could explain what it is they point to. Instead, when Tillich sets out to explain religious symbols, he describes the distinctive way in which they function: religious symbols are distinguished from other representative symbols by the fact that

religious symbols alone directly open up the "ultimate" dimension of reality;

religious symbols alone are bearers of the holy and so "produce the experience of holiness";

religious symbols alone have "healing power."[26]

Religious symbols can be distinguished from other symbols by the unique things they do to men.

26. Ibid., p. 5.

Our contention is that in doing these things religious symbols satisfy the necessary and sufficient conditions for being miracles. They occasion the sudden discernment that the power of being is effectively present in one's life, and they evoke the experience of the holy. To show this, we must examine each of the five characteristics of representative symbols.

Representative symbols open up dimensions of reality and religious representative symbols open up the "ultimate" dimension of reality through things, persons, and events. Ontological analysis, as we shall see in the next chapter, shows that the ultimate dimension of reality is the unconditioned power of being. Since by definition the miracle element in revelatory events mediates the power of being, whatever serves as the giving side may be called a religious symbol. This warrants classifying the biblical picture as a religious symbol.

Religious symbols open up dimensions of reality "which otherwise are covered up by the predominance of other dimensions of . . . reality."[27] They are an occasion for discernment. The fact that Tillich conflates "opening up" in the sense of "mediating" the presence of ultimate reality with "opening up" in the sense of "leading us to discern" suggests that the way in which religious symbols evoke this discernment is an effective mediation of the power of ultimate reality to the man who comes to the·discernment. This further warrants calling the biblical picture a religious symbol, for the picture is said to mediate the power of being by bringing men to discern a particular feature (or dimension) of their own lives, viz., the presence of an unconditioned element.

Religious symbols share with other representative symbols an

27. Ibid.

"integrating" power which is both healing and experienced as holy. If the dimension of reality opened up by religious symbols is the unconditioned power of being, and if the opening up of it is a mediating of power to estranged men, then it is healing. The symbol through which it comes can, accordingly, also be said to have healing powers which integrate both the individual and the religious community to which he belongs.

It follows that a symbol that mediates such power would produce the experience of holiness in persons and groups. As we have seen, that which mediates the ontologically healing power of being is at once shaking and elevating to the man receiving the power. It evokes the experience of holiness. Once again, the defining characteristics of religious symbols are identical with the essential features of miracles. This too warrants calling the picture a religious symbol, since it functions as the miracle element in dependent revelations.

The exposition thus far provides a basis for explicating the three remaining features that religious symbols have in common with all representative symbols: they point beyond themselves; they participate in that to which they point; they cannot be created at will.

Representative symbols, including religious symbols, point beyond themselves. That which opens up the dimension of ultimate reality is not itself the dimension to which it draws attention. This warrants calling the biblical picture a symbol, for the picture depicts Jesus as "negating" himself in order to point to that which transcends him. This is precisely what made him the miracle element in final revelation. There seems to be the implication here that there is some connection between the intrinsic properties of a symbol (e.g. that Jesus' life is characterized by self-negation) and its ability to function in such a way as to point beyond itself.

Like other representative symbols, religious symbols "cannot be created at will." "It is the unconscious–conscious reaction of a *group* through which it becomes a symbol." To be sure, somebody must imaginatively create the symbol. Nevertheless, it has to function in specifiable ways in the life of a group before it can properly be called a representative symbol.

This describes exactly the biblical picture in its role as miracle in dependent revelatory events. As the product of the religious imagination, it expresses the receiving side of the original revelatory event, but it is important to theology only as the giving side of dependent revelations. It fills this role only as it effectively opens up the dimension of ultimate reality or, what is the same thing, as it mediates the power of New Being in a community.

Representative symbols, including religious ones, "participate" in that which they symbolize. This is the most perplexing element in Tillich's theory. He often tries to explain what he means by illustrations:

> the flag participates in the power of the king or nation for which it stands and which it symbolizes. There has, therefore, been a fight since the days of William Tell as to how to behave in the presence of the flag. This would be meaningless if the flag did not participate as a symbol in the power of that which it symbolizes. The whole monarchic idea is itself incomprehensible, if you do not understand that the king always is both: on the one hand, a symbol of the power of the group of which he is the king and on the other hand, he who exercises partly (never fully, of course) this power.[28]

28. Tillich, *Theology of Culture*, p. 55.

The parallel between a king and a symbol is more helpful than the one between a flag and a symbol, though in more abbreviated forms of the argument he usually refers only to the flag.

The point of the parallel lies in the last sentence: "on the one hand, [a king is] a symbol of the power of the group of which he is the king and on the other hand, he [is the one] who exercises partly (never fully, of course) this power." A symbol is a part of a larger, power-bearing whole and is used to point to the whole and to the power that it mediates. It participates in that to which it points in at least two ways, both of them specified in functional terms. For one thing, the symbol participates in the honor, adulation, fear, and the like that is appropriate to the whole of which it is the representative part.

> The representative of a person or institution participates in the honor of those whom he is asked to represent; but it is not *he* who is honored, it is that which or he whom he represents. In this sense we can state generally that the symbol participates in the reality of what it symbolizes.[29]

In the second place, the symbol itself participates in the power mediated by the whole of which it is the representative part in the sense that the power is present in it. It "exercises" the power in some respect.

Since the biblical picture of Jesus as the Christ functions in precisely the same way, it too participates in that to which it points. It is imaginatively created in the occurrence of the original Christian revelation, so its creation is a component element in that event. It is

29. Tillich, "The Meaning and Justification of Religious Symbols," p. 4.

all that remains of that event; hence, it is the part that could represent a larger whole. In dependent Christian revelations, it does exactly that by mediating the same power of being mediated in the original event. Accordingly, it participates in that to which it points. In dependent Christian revelations, it is received with ultimate concern or faith properly due the miracle element of the original revelation, which it merely represents. Properly speaking, it is not itself thereby honored, for the ultimate concern is actually directed toward the unconditioned power of being that is merely given local residence and made concrete by the symbol. As evidence of this, the picture, like the one it pictures, negates itself. So too, the picture participates in the power of New Being just as much as the receiver of the picture does.

This exposition of Tillich's remarks about representative symbols throws light on his repeated claim that religious symbols are untranslatable. In his earliest essay, he defended this claim by saying that religious symbols have "innate power."[30] This phrase suggested a quasi-magical view of symbols. In more recent discussions, he has abandoned this approach. Instead of arguing their untranslatability on the grounds of their ontological nature, he supports it by analysis of the peculiar function representative symbols fill. They function in man's communal life by representing larger wholes having special significance and power over men's lives. Tillich's argument may be glossed in the following way. There are certain very complex events that are important to the men involved in them. The mind cannot easily entertain these events in all their complexity if it uses abstract categories to map all their features in a systematic and discursive way. Consequently, men use a recognizable part of the whole that can imaginatively be seen as representing, in a con-

30. Tillich, "The Religious Symbol," pp. 3–4; cf. p. 16.

crete way, the whole in all its complexity. According to some critics, this is what images do in well-wrought poetry.[31] It also occurs in popular and folk history. A single event in a highly complex historical occurrence is taken imaginatively as representing the whole in all its complexity. Abraham Lincoln, for example, has clearly become the popular representative symbol for the American Civil War, representing in his life and tragic death the greater complexities and ambiguities of the entire historical episode. Such a historical representative symbol does not express historical truth that could be verified empirically, but it does give an expression to those features of the entire historical event that American society takes to be important, and thus it gives a focal point by reference to which the significance or importance of other events can be rated. It cannot, then, be "translated" into straight historical narrative. Similarly, a religious symbol like the biblical picture does not express "truths" but serves to express those features of a revelatory event with which the faithful are especially, indeed "ultimately," concerned. It provides a norm by which other such events can be rated, and it cannot be translated into another mode of discourse, such as ontology or history.

Tillich's analysis of the dynamics of revelation provides the warrants for theological judgments about religious symbols and for his general theory of religious symbols. This may be considered an exercise in the philosophy of religion, but it is not ontological anal-

31. E.g. John Donne's use of the conceit of the compass in "A Valediction Forbidding Mourning" and Tate's comments on it. Also see the discussion of *Paradiso*, Canto 23 in Dante's *The Divine Comedy*, in Alan Tate, *The Man of Letters in the Modern World* (New York, Meridian Books, 1958), pp. 93–112. See also Cleanth Brooks and Robert Penn Warren (*Understanding Poetry* [New York, Henry Holt & Co., 1950]) on Andrew Marvell's "The Definition of Love" (pp. 293–97), and on Amy Lowell's "Patterns" (pp. 55–61).

ysis. While Tillich appeals to Scripture for his data and for some of the backing for his warrants, the warrants themselves are gotten from his philosophy of religion.

This philosophical account of religious experience, however, does not provide a criterion by which to distinguish the symbols expressing religious experiences from those expressing revelations. It may tell a theologian what he may say about symbols expressing the content of a revelation, but it cannot help him determine which symbols he ought to explicate. Yet Tillich himself introduces this as an important distinction for the theologian to make. He wants to protect the "otherness" or "givenness" or revelation, so that its content will not be explained in terms of sociological factors or in terms of chemical or psychological imbalances in those who receive what is given in revelation. He wants to contend that the symbols expressing a revelation are somehow grasped by the deliberate agency of the power of being which "expresses *itself* in symbols and myths" (*ST, 1,* 110).[32]

If it were possible, independently of religious symbols, to describe what is manifested in revelation, then perhaps it would be possible to determine which religious symbols express that content and which do not. An obvious candidate for this job is Tillich's ontology. In the next chapter, we shall try to discover what role ontological speculation plays in the fabric of his theological argument.

32. For an important discussion of both the history and confusions in Tillich's doctrine concerning religious symbols, see Lewis S. Ford, "The Three Strands of Tillich's Theory of Religious Symbols," *Journal of Religion, 46,* Pt. 2 (January 1966), 104–30. Ford distinguishes between the religious and the metaphysical roles Tillich makes symbols play, and his discussion of the religious role has some affinities as well as some important differences with the discussion given above.

3

THE ROLE OF ONTOLOGICAL ANALYSIS

Tillich's account of the nature of ontology makes it clear that one thing it cannot do is describe that which is manifested in revelation. Ontological analysis can show why men quest for a kind of ontological healing, and it can show how such healing might take place in revelatory occurrences, but it cannot describe the "transcendent" reality that does this healing. It can show why ontological healing comes only when a concrete holy object is conjoined with the "religious a priori," but it cannot show why one finite entity does in fact become a holy object occasioning a saving discernment for me while some other finite entity does not. Furthermore, it cannot show with respect to any particular alleged revelatory occurrence that the unconditioned power of being was truly mediated there.

What ontological argument can do is provide warrants for the warrants used in first-level theological argument. Theological argument moves to conclusions about biblical religious symbols. The warrants for these moves consist in generalizations about revelatory occurrences whose backings are descriptions of particular revelatory events. We may call this first-level argument. If someone asks for justification for the move from the proffered backing to the warrants used in first-level argument, a new second-level argument would have to be constructed. Here, the backing of the first-level argument would be the data and the warrants the conclusions. This is where Tillich's ontological analysis fits in. It provides the warrants used in second-level argument to justify the move from the backing to the warrants of first-level argument.

The Limits of Ontological Analysis

According to Tillich, ontological analysis gives a descriptive account of some features of finite reality. It can also point out the fact that some unconditional elements are present in finite entities. But ontological analysis can yield no information about any realm of reality that "transcends" finite reality. Tillich expressly says that it cannot yield the doctrine of God; that only comes from revelation (*ST, 1*, 243).

Tillich takes "life" rather than "being" as the most inclusive and ultimate "ontological concept" (*ST, 3*, 11, 12). He introduces it in Part IV of the system where he discusses concrete actuality in all its complexity. "Being" is used to designate a "power inherent in everything" by which each thing "resists" all that threatens to destroy it.[1] Tillich discusses "being" in the first and second parts of the system, for it designates a feature of the essential aspect of reality abstracted from concrete actuality. "Life," however, designates the "actuality of being," i.e. concrete actuality where essential and existential aspects are mixed. Tillich thinks that, used in this way, the concept "life" is liberated from its "bondage to the organic realm. It designates the process of actualization of potentiality that occurs in all realms of reality. Tillich prefers the term

1. Cf. *ST, 1*, 163–64.

"life" to "process" because it more clearly expresses the fact that this process is a process of conquering its own built-in negations (*ST*, *3*, 11–12).

Although he never expressly says so, all of Tillich's discussion of the real world (actuality) suggests that he thinks of it as a vast network of interrelated, interdependent, but irreducibly individual "life processes" or "lives." In Tillich's terms, actual life is always "centered." This is evidenced, for example, by Tillich's analysis of life into three functions. Life entails "self-integration." In the process of life, "the center of self-identity is established, drawn into self-alteration and re-established with the contents of that into which it has been altered." Simultaneously, life entails "self-creation." "Life drives toward the new. It cannot do this without centeredness, but it does it by transcending every individual center." "One finite situation is transcended by another, but finite life itself is not transcended." Thirdly, "Life drives beyond itself as finite life." In this function, life is constantly "driving toward the sublime" where sublimity points to a "going beyond limits" (*ST*, *3*, 30–31). In each of these, a basic structure of self-identity and self-alteration in life is effective. Clearly, instead of saying that life entails these functions, Tillich could have said less misleadingly that each "life process" or simply each "life" entails them.[2]

One feature of life in its essential (as opposed to existential) aspect is its variety of dimensions. Tillich notes the inorganic, organic, self-aware, spiritual, and historical dimensions, but says that there is no definite number of dimensions. These dimensions are all present, actually or potentially, in all life. There can be no

2. The ontology Tillich sketched in *Love, Power, and Justice* (New York, Oxford University Press, 1954) supports this judgment.

mutual interference among them. Conflicts that threaten the unity of life arise, not from these essential distinctions within life, but from existential disruption of all of life. In man, whose life is dominated by the historical dimension, all dimensions are in principle fully actualized and unified. His life includes the inorganic and organic dimensions, in virtue of his body; the dimension of self-awareness, in virtue of his psychological makeup; the spiritual dimension, in virtue of his capacity to combine power and meaning in free inter-personal activity; and the historical dimension, in virtue of his participation in communities whose ongoing histories are lived as having intention and purpose (*ST, 3,* 15–28).[3]

As is characteristic of Tillich's discussions of the essential aspect of actuality, his discussion of life's dimensions uses "life" in a dis-tinctly monistic way. He talks of the "multidimensional unity of life," with stress on the "unity," as though life were the only really real "substance" and all distinctions among modes of life and disjunctions between individual lives were merely apparent. A more consistent explication of Tillich's ontology can be given if we read what he says about life's essential aspect in the context of what he says about it as concrete actuality. Read this way, he is simply claiming that it is an essential feature of each "life process" to include a number of dimensions without prejudice to its "centered-ness" or unity.

The three-part structure of life is dependent on the essential "structures of being." Tillich gives a sketch of these structures in Part II of the system where he discusses the essential aspect of concrete actuality. It too has an occasional monistic sound that

3. Cf. *ST, 3,* 300–13.

must be discounted by reading it in the context of his fuller account of actuality.

Since all dimensions of life are most fully actual in man, Tillich develops his account of the structures of being by doing an onto-logical analysis of man's life (*ST, 1,* 168–69). There is a curious shift of focus as one moves from Tillich's systematically primary account of actuality, i.e. of life, to his systematically secondary account of the essential structures of being. The discussion of life is cast in terms of what life processes do to themselves, so to speak: *self*-integration, *self*-creation, *self*-transcendence. The account of the structures of being, however, is done in terms of what the world does to man and what man does to the world. The structures of being are identified by an analysis of the a priori conditions of experience (*ST, 1,* 166).[4] The conditions of experience constitute the most general features of reality precisely because everything that is experienced or experienceable is experienced in terms of those conditions.[5] Consequently, the concepts yielded by analysis of the conditions of experience are predicable of all actual things (i.e. life processes) whatsoever.

Tillich suggests that there are "four levels of ontological concepts" (*ST, 1,* 164)[6] that together describe the ontological structures of finite realities. The first and basic one is the fact that all experience involves a "self" and a "world." This may be stated more abstractly as the subject–object polarity and is the necessary condition in the essential scheme of things for the dual acts of self-identity and self-alteration which are effective in the three functions that constitute

---

4. Cf. *Dynamics of Faith,* p. 90; *Love, Power, and Justice,* p. 23.
5. Cf. *ST, 1,* 164, 167; *Biblical Religion,* p. 8.
6. See also *Biblical Religion,* pp. 13, 19.

life processes.[7] The three subsequent levels of ontological concepts seemed to be progressively more precise specifications of this basic structure.

The second level of ontological concepts consists in three pairs of "polar elements": individuality and participation, dynamics and form, freedom and destiny. They are qualities of all actual being and are not themselves transempirical "beings"; they are always found in pairs.

> The first element expresses the self-relatedness of [each actual] being, its power of being something for itself, while the second element expresses the belongingness of being, its character of being a part of the universe of being (*ST, 1*, 165).

Individuality and participation together designate the a priori conditions for "life's function of self-integration" (*ST, 3*, 32–33). A fully individualized entity is a fully centered or integrated one. At the same time, it is an entity capable of the profoundest sort of relatedness to other entities. When this is stated in the dynamic terms of life, it means that a fully individualized life process is one that preserves its centeredness precisely through its participation in other life processes: it is self-integrating. Dynamics and form together designate the a priori condition for life's function of self-growth. In growth, a "formed reality goes beyond itself to another form [dynamics], which both preserves and transforms the original reality [form]" (*ST, 3*, 50–51). Freedom and destiny designate the a priori conditions of life's function of self-transcendence. Destiny designates the limited, finite givenness of each life process, and freedom its ceaseless straining to escape bondage to its own finitude

7. Cf. *ST, 1*, 164, 168–71; *3*, 32.

(*ST, 3,* 86–87). If one is to give an adequate ontological account of anything, he must use these three sets of terms to specify both the peculiar ways in which it is what it is independently of its relations to other things (is a "self") and the peculiar ways in which it is what it is only in virtue of its relations to other things (is part of a "world").

The third level of ontological concepts expresses "the difference between essential and existential being" and describes the a priori conditions allowing that difference to arise. In his *Systematic Theology,* Tillich seems most regularly to use "essential being" to refer to "created reality," and "existential being" to refer to a "distortion of essential being" (*ST, 1,* 202–04).[8] The a priori conditions that allow this contrast to arise are exhibited by an analysis "of finitude in its polarity with infinity as well as in its relation to freedom and destiny, to being and non-being, to essence and existence" (*ST, 1,* 165).

The fourth level of ontological concepts deals "with those concepts which traditionally have been called the categories, that is the basic forms of thought and being, "the forms in which the mind grasps and shapes reality." They are "time," "space," "cause," and "substance" (*ST, 1,* 82, 165, 192–97). All experiencing, thinking, and imagining is done in terms of them. Each thing is experienced and thought of as "contingent"[9] because the particular time, space, cause, and substance to which reference is made might logically have been different. By definition this means that anything experienced (or thought or imagined) is finite, for "the categories of ex-

8. Cf. ibid., *2,* 24–26.
9. Paul Tillich, *The Courage To Be* (New Haven, Yale University Press, 1952), p. 144.

perience are the categories of finitude." It also means that the experiencing (or thinking or imagining) subject or "reason" is finite. It is bound to these categories and cannot grasp and shape reality in any other terms. Consequently, man cannot grasp reality-in-itself but rather is limited to grasping his world, i.e. "the totality of the phenomena which appear to him and which constitute his actual experience" (*ST, 1,* 81–82).

The categories are the forms not only of experience "from the outside, namely in relation to the world" but also " 'from the inside,' namely, in relation to the self." The result is that one always experiences oneself as limited temporally, spatially, causally, and substantively. This mode of experience is called "anxiety." It is an awareness that in all of these respects one is oneself "contingent" and "transitory" (*ST, 1,* 193).[10] Thus, all known and knowable beings are known as finite, i.e. known in terms of the categories. It is in this respect that it can be said that the categories are the basic forms not only of thought but also of being.

These four levels of ontological categories designate the a priori conditions of experience yielded by an analysis of the structures of experience. They clearly limit any inquiry, including ontology, to describing finite entities only. Despite this limitation, ontological analysis can draw attention to the presence of "unconditional elements" in finite men's lives. The elements are unconditional in that they are "noumena" that cannot be experienced or known in terms of the categories. Since all experiencing and knowing is done in terms of the categories, this means that what the unconditional elements are cannot be known. Nevertheless, Tillich thinks it pos-

10. See also ibid., p. 42.

sible to draw attention to the sheer fact that something unconditional, an "x"-we-know-not-what, is present.

For example, the power in finite things designated by the term "being" is an unconditional element. Finite things are limited in ways specified by the categories, and these limits are threats to the perduring of the entities.[11] Nevertheless, finite realities continue to evidence a power to be in spite of the threats. When he speaks of this power in general terms, Tillich calls it the power of "being-itself" (*ST, 1,* 164, 189). When it is thought of as effective in particular things it is said to be the power of being in those things.[12]

11. Cf. *ST, 1,* 196.

12. Cf. ibid., pp. 189, 191, 195–96, 203. As John Macquarrie has pointed out, the phrase "power of being" is doubly ambiguous. The word "being" in the phrase may be used either as it is used in the phrase "being-itself" or as it is used in the phrase "ground of being." These must be quite different uses of "being." "Being" as used in "being-itself" can, as an ultimate, have no "ground," while "being" as used in "ground of being" must refer to individual (and so finite) entities. It seems to me clear that Tillich uses "being" in the phrase "power of being" in the same way as in the phrase "being-itself." It is not itself a particular being, which would necessarily be a "finite" being. Rather it is a way of indicating the presence of an "unconditional" element within finite entities, an "x"-we-know-not-what. The second ambiguity in the use of the term "being" is in the phrase "power exerted by being" or the "power to be." Inasmuch as the "power of being" is explicitly treated as an "unconditional" element present in finite objects, but neither as part of the "structure" of finite entities nor as explicable on the basis of resources intrinsic to finite entities, it seems to me fair to conclude that Tillich means the "power to be." Although it is found *in* finite entities, it is not, properly speaking, their own, self-generated power which they exert autonomously ("power exerted by being" where "being" means an indefinite range of finite entities). Macquarrie seems to me unduly perplexed by these ambiguities. They resolve themselves fairly quickly once it is clear that for Tillich "being" does not designate a "highest being" or "most abstract and all-inclusive category" or "the most pervasive structure that can be found in finite entities," but rather simply "power to resist threats." Cf. John Macquarrie, *Twentieth-Century Religious Thought* (New York, Harper & Row, 1963), p. 367, n. 26.

In neither case is "being" the name for a describable feature of actuality. It certainly is not the name for the "highest abstraction," i.e. the name for whatever is left after one has subtracted all features that are peculiar to any range of reality.[13] Rather, it is a way of referring to a recurrent experience. "It is the expression of the experience of being over against non-being" (*ST, 2,* 11). That whose presence is experienced, i.e. the "power" itself, cannot itself be perceived or known because it is not "conditioned" by the categories in terms of which all perception and knowledge are cast. All that the term "being" does is signal the fact that this unconditional element is present.[14]

Behind this account of the logical status of the term "being" is the fact that Tillich begins ontological analysis with an analysis of human experience. The "experience of being over against non-being" is a human experience. A man realizes in shock that he is persistently threatened by biological extinction, cognitive skepticism, and moral nihilism. At the same time, he finds he has the power to engage in acts of self-affirmation by which he wards off threats to the biological, intellectual, and moral aspects of his personal life. This is the experience of the presence of the power of being in human life.

It is very important to notice that Tillich explicitly identifies the power of being in man with the "courage to be"[15] It is this identifi-

---

13. Cf. *ST, 1,* 163–64.

14. Tillich contends that the so-called "ontological argument" for the existence of God is not an argument at all but an analysis of finite being designed to point out the presence of the "unconditioned" within the realm of the finite (ibid., p. 206).

15. Cf. Tillich, *The Courage To Be,* pp. 72, 181; *ST, 1,* 253.

cation that turns Tillich's ontology into a philosophical anthropology: "We have defined courage as the self-affirmation of being in spite of non-being. The power of this self-affirmation *is* the power of being which is effective in every act of courage."[16]

To this, one more point needs to be added. Tillich sometimes talks as though ontology's task was to discover the answer to the question, Why is there something rather than nothing? (*ST, 1,* 110, 113, 163) However, Tillich admits that as a straightforward question this is meaningless, "for every possible answer would be subject to the same question in an infinite regression." The question does not make a request for information; it is an expression of one's "state of existence rather than . . . a formulated question." The state of existence expressed in the question is the state of estrangement from the power of being. This estrangement leads to the loss of the "courage to be." In an effort to regain the power of being, "reason reaches its boundary line, is thrown back upon itself [for the very reason that the unconditioned power of being is beyond the boundary imposed on knowledge by the categories], and then is driven again to its extreme situation." This is experienced in extreme anxiety as a shock (*ST, 1,* 163–64).[17] Tillich seems to be saying that the ontological question is not so much a request for information as an involuntary "ouch" expressing an ontological pain. The question, of course, cannot be treated as a serious request for new knowledge precisely because it arises "when reason is driven beyond itself" (*ST, 1,* 110), i.e. beyond the limits of what it can know. No philosophical doctrine of God need be developed to answer it, and none can be.

16. Tillich, *The Courage To Be,* p. 172 (my italics).
17. Cf. *ST, 1,* 113.

The Ontology of the Self

Ontology cannot contribute to theology an independent account of that which is manifested in revelation, but the fact that ontology entails a philosophical anthropology allows it to fill a quite different role in theological argument. It can provide warrants for the warrants used in drawing theological conclusions about the biblical picture of Jesus as the Christ. We have seen that these warrants consist in generalizations about revelatory occurrences. Tillich's ontological analysis of the self can support these generalizations by showing why men quest for a kind of ontological healing and by showing how such healing takes place in revelatory occurrences. It can also show why ontological healing only comes when a concrete holy object is conjoined with a religious a priori.

According to Tillich, one's "being" as a self is "essentially threatened." "It can be lost or saved" (*ST, 1,* 14). The possibility of loss of selfhood is a feature of the essential aspect of actual selves and is not the result of existential corruption of the self. Whether or not the self is lost depends on whether or not it has the power of being or, what is the same thing, the courage to be. Much of Tillich's ontology suggests that whether or not man has the courage to be depends on his being able to use his reason in a certain way. It depends on whether he is able to use his reason so as to be aware, during the course of its use, of unconditional absolutes. To have this certainty is to have the courage to be and to have ontological "health"; to lack it is to lose the courage to be and to fall into ontological "disease." Tillich never explicitly makes this connection between a particular way of using reason and the courage to be, but the relation is implied by much that he says.

Throughout this discussion, Tillich's extremely broad definition of reason needs to be kept in mind. Reason is "the structure of the mind which enables it to grasp and shape reality." Grasping and shaping go on in a whole range of reciprocal transactions between self and "other," including "cognitive, aesthetic, practical, and technical" transactions (*ST, 1,* 72, 75). Tillich regularly uses "spiritual" or "creative" to refer to the use of reason to grasp and shape either one's self or one's world.[18] As the structure that makes this range of transaction possible, reason clearly includes, but is more than, the ability to reason or to calculate means for ends. This more narrow (and familiar) use of reason is "technical reason." It is not to be confused with the broader use of reason as "ontological reason" (*ST, 1,* 71–75) which is the sense of the term used here.

According to Tillich, the structure of reason consists of three sets of paired elements, each of which is found without exception in all the ways in which mind and reality interact. For our purposes the most important pair of elements is structure and depth. Structure is never clearly defined. It seems to refer to the orderliness ingredient in any act of grasping and shaping and so includes the categories and the laws governing valid argument (*ST, 1,* 84). Tillich's description of the "depth" of reason is even more mystifying:

> The depth of reason is the *expression* of something that *is not reason* [where "reason" means "the structure of the mind which enables it to grasp and shape reality" (*ST, 1,* 75)] but which precedes reason and is manifest *through* it. Reason in both its objective and its subjective structures points to something which appears in these structures but which transcends them in power

18. Cf. *ST, 1,* 180; *The Courage To Be,* p. 46; *ST, 1,* 15, n. 1; *3,* 22.

and meaning. *This is not another field of reason* which could be progressively discovered and expressed, but is that which is expressed *through* every rational expression. It could be called . . . "being itself" which is manifest in the *logos* of being.

. . .

In the cognitive realm the depth of reason is its quality of pointing to "truth-itself," namely to the infinite power of being and of the ultimately real, through the relative truths in every field of knowledge. In the aesthetic realm the depth of reason is its quality of pointing to "beauty-itself," namely to an infinite meaning and ultimate significance, through the creations in every field of aesthetic intuition. (*ST, 1,* 79; my italics)

Some sense can be made of this if we follow Tillich's hint and take the depth of reason to be his equivalent for the "absolutes" or "ultimate principles" in the thirteenth-century Franciscan development of Augustinian religious epistemology. According to Tillich, this school held that "ultimate principles and knowledge of them are independent of the changes and relativities of the individual mind. . . . The principles are not created functions of our mind, but the presence of truth itself and therefore of God, *in* our mind."[19] God's "presence" in man's mind, or within reason's structure, is a necessary condition of all thought, for thought, according to this argument, aims at truth and so its attempts to know require attempts at judging the truth of sentences expressing one's thoughts. But judgments of truth suppose a standard of truth which is knowable and in fact applied. Men, after all, do argue and come to agreement

19. Tillich, *Theology of Culture*, p. 13; cf. *ST, 3,* 126–27.

about the truth of judgments of value; hence, there must be a common standard which is actually used. However, men could not individually have invented this standard or, the argument runs, it would be private to each man and so finally useless in helping men come to common agreement about truth. Moreover (and here Tillich's own analysis of finitude comes into play), the limits on man's reason are such that he could never have come to know this standard, for all learning and all experiencing are limited by the categories which make all learned knowledge in principle doubtable. But the absolute and common standards by which judgments of truth are made cannot themselves be doubted. They are not relative but absolute, i.e. "without relation"; they themselves are not subject to evaluation on the basis of some further canon. Instead, all else are relative to them, i.e. judged (e.g. as to "truth" or "beauty") by the relation of "approximation to" which they have to the absolute.[20] This is what it means to say that the absolutes are not created by the mind but are the presence of God in the mind. Tillich seems to say the same thing about "truth-itself," "beauty-itself," etc., when he says that they are instances of something appearing in reason's structure but transcending that structure:

> This [realm of the transcendent within reason; i.e. reason's depth] is not another field of reason which could progressively be discovered and expressed, but is that which is expressed through every rational expression. It could be called . . . "being-itself" which is manifest in the *logos* of being. (*ST, 1,* 79)

In short, *the depth of reason is the presence of the unconditioned in man's reason.* Tillich identifies this with the presence of the Spirit

20. Tillich, *Theology of Culture,* p. 24.

to man's spirit (*ST*, *3*, 113). More precisely, it is the effective functioning of the unconditioned in the acts in which one exercises reason. We say the "effective functioning" because one is able to engage in those acts of grasping and shaping only by selecting norms and goals. This in turn requires value judgments, and *that* can be done only if one has some purchase on the absolutes or norms for guiding such judgments.[21]

The connection between using reason with an awareness of its depth and preserving one's ontological well-being is implied in two different discussions Tillich gives of the ontology of the self—its existential disruption and its healing or salvation. In his *Systematic Theology*, Tillich contends that the distinctively "human" thing about "human being" is the peculiar way that man is related in two different relations. Both relations can be disrupted; this is their essential threatenedness. Both relations are functions of man's rea-

21. Further corroboration of this interpretation of Tillich's notion of the "depth of reason" is provided by his remarks on the "ontological argument" for the existence of God. Far from being an argument, it is a way of pointing out "the presence within finitude of an element which transcends it." This element, Tillich goes on to say, "is experienced both theoretically and practically. The theoretical side has been elaborated by Augustine, the practical side by Kant" (*ST*, *1*, 206). Judging by the reference, it seems fair to conclude that the "practical" experience of the unconditioned which Kant has elaborated is the experience of what Tillich calls "the unconditional element in the moral imperative" (*ST*, *1*, 207). The reference to Augustine suggests, of course, that the "theoretical" experience is precisely the experience we have been discussing, viz., the experience of exercising one's powers of "grasping and shaping" self and world on the basis of some apprehension of the "absolutes." Still further support for this reading of Tillich comes in his discussion of the presence of the Spirit of God in man's life, or "Spiritual Presence," as he calls it, when he identifies "Spiritual Presence" with what the "Franciscan theologians of the thirteenth century insisted" was "the divine character of the principles of truth in the human mind" (*ST*, *3*, 126).

son. The health of the relations, and so of the self they constitute, depends on the condition of man's reason.

First, to be "human" is to be "centered" or to be a self.[22] The basis of this is the relation one has to one's self in "self-consciousness." On the basis of self-consciousness one is a "centered" being, i.e. a being whose "reaction to a stimulus is dependent on a structural whole." Man is a complex whole organized out of parts, many of which are capable of semi-autonomous action. However, he is such a highly integrated whole that as a whole he is able to regulate his action as an integrated being and subordinate the activities of his several parts to his action as a whole being. He is able to criticize his own activity, apprehend the character of the context within which he must act, identify diverse demands on himself for various courses of action, and plan and effect alterations in his activity. Insofar as man is free to do these things, he does them by exercising his reason.

Second, to be "human" is to have a world. This is not simply man's environment, i.e. "those things with which [he] has an active interrelation." Man "transcends every possible environment." He has a world which "is the structural whole which includes and transcends all environments," both actual and imaginable. A man's world is a perspective in which the man organizes (structures) the multitude of actual and imaginable things he encounters, including even himself, giving them a unity simply because they are organized in *his* perspective. This is the way man is related to what is other than himself. It is a function of his rationality, his ability to grasp and shape reality "according to universal norms and ideas."

22. For what follows, see ibid., *1*, 169–71, 259.

These two modes of relation are inseparable precisely because they both are functions of reason. Without a consciousness of a world, "self-consciousness would have no content, for every content, psychic as well as bodily, lies within the universe. There is no self-consciousness without world-consciousness." Conversely, "world-consciousness is possible only on the basis of a fully developed self-consciousness." Only the fully self-related (self-conscious) being is free enough of itself as given in and by an environment to be free also of the environment and so be able to have a world.

What is most important is that these two inseparable modes of relation are functions of reason. Man is related to himself and the world only by exercising his reason. He must actually grasp and shape both himself and his world in order to be related to either. If his grasping and shaping is to be significant, it must be done by reference to the absolutes, i.e. the depth of reason. It is not so much the having of reason as the proper using of it that constitutes the ontological health of the self.

Conversely, it ought to be the case that ontological disruption of the self follows from an inability to use reason with full awareness of its depth. This is quite clearly implied both in Tillich's description of the cause of ontological disruption and in his account of how ontological disruption comes about.

The cause of the self's ontological disruption is estrangement from the power of being itself. The central element in estrangement is "unbelief." By "unbelief" Tillich does not mean "disbelief" in certain claims but rather "unfaith" (*ST, 2,* 47).[23] In one place

23. If "estrangement" is understood to be "unfaith" (i.e. "unbelief"), then it must also be understood as "hubris" and "concupiscence." "Hubris" is that denial of one's finitude (ibid., 2, 50) which is implied in any awareness of one's

Tillich defines faith as one's consciousness "of the Spiritual Presence's work in him" (*ST, 3,* 133). Unfaith would be the absence of this awareness. Consequently, in this (rather special) sense, "unbelief is the disruption of man's *cognitive* participation in God" (*ST, 2,* 47).

Perhaps the best way to get at what he means is by inference from his descriptions of the results of losing this cognition. If man were not estranged, he would live "in the power of the dimension of the eternal" and by that power could accept all his "insecurity and uncertainty." But,

> in the state of estrangement the dimension of the ultimate is shut off. . . . Insecurity becomes absolute and drives toward a despair about the possibility of being at all. Doubt becomes absolute and drives toward a despairing refusal to accept any finite truth. (*ST, 2,* 73)

The context makes it clear that the "dimension of the ultimate" is being "shut off" from the set of acts in which one uses reason. The passage makes it clear that the result of shutting the "ultimate" off

---

own power-of-being unaccompanied by a correlative awareness that this power is *identical* with the power of being-itself, i.e. lacks an awareness that its power is not self-generated. And "concupiscence" is the consequence of this, viz., acting as though one's own power of being could control *all* finite beings (cf. ibid., p. 52). All three (unbelief, hubris, concupiscence) are involved in "estrangement" from the power of being-itself. But the way Tillich relates "hubris" and "concupiscence" to "unbelief" indicates that in some way they depend on or result from "unbelief." The loss of "awareness," i.e. "unbelief," seems to be the act in which "hubris" and "concupiscence," which are actual possibilities for man precisely because he is essentially "individual" (understood in polar relation with "Participant") and "centered," become actualized in a man's life.

from those acts is to destroy all confidence in the validity or meaningfulness of those acts. On the basis of these observations it seems
fair to gloss "dimension of the ultimate" with "depth of reason."
The depth of reason is the presence of unconditioned elements in
one's reason. "Ultimate dimension" and "unconditioned" seem to be
interchangeable terms. Furthermore, the depth of reason functions
in those intellectual acts as the absolutes by reference to which one
makes value judgments. If one were to lose awareness of those
absolutes, one could not engage in that kind of use of reason with
any sense of meaningfulness. Value judgments, whether of truth
values or moral values or aesthetic values or pragmatic values, would
all seem arbitrary and endlessly debatable. One would refuse to
accept as true any finite value judgment at all. This is precisely what
happens when the dimension of the ultimate is shut off from the acts
in which one uses reason "creatively."

In short, the cognition by which one has a "cognitive participation
in God" simply is that immediate awareness of the depth of reason
that underlies discussion about relative value judgments. It is the
consciousness of the Spiritual Presence at work in one's spiritual
activity, i.e. one's use of reason. Hence, estrangement from God is
simply the loss of this consciousness or awareness.

As a direct result of estrangement, man's basic ontological structure turns into a "structure of destruction."[24] The two relations
constituting his "being" simultaneously tend toward dissolution.
Although Tillich does not explicitly make the connection, it seems
clear from his account of the self-destruction of the estranged man
that the process of destruction results from a disruption of man's
reason. When one ceases being aware of the presence of the un-

24. For what follows, see ibid., pp. 60–63.

conditioned absolutes in one's use of reason, then the rational acts in which one relates oneself to both one's self and one's world become unfree. The result is a loss of "centeredness" and a loss of one's world.

Self-loss is "the disintegration of the centered self by disruptive drives which cannot be brought into unity . . . and split the person." It comes with the disruption of that relation to oneself in which one is able to coordinate all of the diverse drives and interests of the self into a coherent whole. This disruption is most evident in the way in which the self's freedom and destiny tend to separate. Freedom and destiny constitute one set of the polar elements that make up the second level of ontological concepts; that is to say, they designate two aspects of the complex relation between self and world. Freedom unguided by a certain apprehension of its own norm, viz., destiny, becomes "arbitrariness" and "ceases to relate itself to objects provided by destiny. It relates itself to an indefinite number of contents. When man makes himself the center of the universe, freedom loses its definiteness." So too, "destiny is distorted into mechanical necessity." Destiny is "myself as *given,* formed by nature, history, and myself" (*ST, 1,* 185; my italics). However, in estrangement one part of what a man is in the present moment is taken to be the norm for action; thereby, one part of destiny dominates the rest of the man in a compulsion. "What seems to be free proves to be conditioned by internal compulsions and external causes" (*ST, 2,* 67). This disruption of the relation between freedom and destiny comes when reason is so disrupted that when man uses it he no longer has confidence that he has a valid immediate apprehension of the "moral norm which, if obeyed, would preserve his essential structure."[25]

25. Tillich, *The Courage To Be,* p. 54.

This is to lose an immediate awareness of the presence, in one's acts of making moral judgments, of "the unconditional element in the moral imperative" (*ST, 1*, 207). Loss of "centeredness" is a disruption of man's self-relation that comes when man loses awareness of the presence in his rational acts of the unconditioned absolutes.

Estrangement from the power of being is an ontological break because it involves the ontological disruption of the self. But the ontological break is a function of a cognitive break; the disruption in the ontological relation between man and the unconditioned is a function of a disruption in the cognitive relation between man and the unconditioned, and not the other way around. When man is estranged, he suffers not just self-loss but also world-loss.

World-loss is the dissolution of "the structural whole" made of all possible environments, actual and imaginable and united by being the perspective of one self. The structural whole "ceases to be a world, in the sense of a *meaningful whole*. Things no longer speak to man; they lose their power to enter into a meaningful encounter with man, because man himself has lost this power" (*ST, 2*, 61). Loss of a world comes when one's relation to that which is other than one's self is disrupted. It seems clear that this disruption comes when man's relation to meanings is disrupted. This is precisely what happens when man loses an awareness of the effective presence of the unconditioned in his spiritual activity.

Clearly, since the two modes of relation (relation to self and relation to what is other than self) are interrelated, the disruption of one also entails the disruption of the other. To the extent that the self undergoes the experience of "falling to pieces," one's world also "falls to pieces." Both result from a loss of confidence in one's apprehension of the absolutes, the presence of the unconditioned in one's exercise of reason.

In *The Courage To Be,* Tillich gives a second account of the ontology of the self in which the self's well-being is made to depend on its proper use of reason. As we have seen, the courage to be is the mode in which the power of being is present in man. It is that which "determines our having or not having distinctively *human* being," i.e. "the whole of human reality" (*ST, 1,* 14). The "whole of human reality" includes three distinct classes of activity. In each, man is threatened in a special way and is aware of the threat in a special anxiety. When a man has courage, he continues to act in each of these three aspects of life in spite of the threats. He exercises the power of being that resists the threats of nonbeing.

The first aspect of human "being" is man's "simple existence,"[26] the biological life. In the "anxiety of death" one is aware of the finitude of simple existence; one is aware of the threatening possibility of "the complete loss of self which biological extinction implies." However, the man with courage "affirms himself ontically" in spite of this threat. Apparently this means that he has the courage to continue planning and acting toward valued goals despite the fact that his physical finitude makes such planning seem foolish and devoid of lasting "meaning and purpose."

The second aspect of human "being" is man's "creativity" or his ability to live "in the various spheres of meanings." Tillich calls this "spiritual" activity, i.e. the use of reason to grasp and shape reality. In the "anxiety of meaninglessness" one is aware of the threatening possibility of a total loss of meaning in one's spiritual life. One is

26. For what follows, see ibid., pp. 42–53; *ST, 1,* 193.

"cut off from creative participation in a sphere of culture" or "driven from devotion to one object to devotion to another and again on to another, because the meaning of each of them vanishes." However, the man with courage "affirms himself spiritually"; he is able to continue in creative activities in spite of this threat.

The third aspect of human "being" is man's ability "to determine himself through decisions in the center of his being" and thereby arrive at the aim of existence, viz., the "actualization of what he potentially is." Whereas the first aspect of the "whole of human reality" consisted in acts related to satisfying physical needs and the second consisted in spiritual acts, this aspect consists in "moral" acts. According to Tillich's analysis, any truly free act is an act by a truly "centered self." It is done by a man able to act as an integrated whole. The whole which he now is is his destiny. Destiny is "not a strange power which determines what shall happen to me. It is myself as given, formed by nature, history, and myself. My destiny is the basis of my freedom; my freedom participates in shaping my destiny."[27] This means that any truly free act, as the act of one's "centered totality," is an act done on the basis of one's whole destiny and not on the basis of just part of it. In the "anxiety of guilt"[28] a man is aware of the threatening possibility of acting in such a way as to contradict his essential being and thereby lose his destiny. However, the man with courage "affirms himself morally." Evidently this means that he is able to continue to act in spite of the threat of acting in a self-destructive way.

Tillich insists that these three aspects of the "whole of human reality" are inseparably intertwined. The anxieties are "immanent"

27. Tillich, *The Courage To Be*, p. 185; cf. *ST*, 2, 42–43.
28. See Tillich, *The Courage To Be*, pp. 51–53, 61.

in one another; the correlative modes of courage, though distinguishable, are not separable. This brings us once more to the crux of the argument. Although he does not say it explicitly, Tillich implicitly makes the courage of spiritual self-affirmation basic to the others and hence basic to the "being" of the total self. The courage of spiritual self-affirmation, in turn, depends on the ability to use reason in full awareness of its depth. Here too, the ontological health of the self has been shown to be dependent on the proper use of reason.

Tillich regularly describes the courage to affirm oneself as a *"confidence."*[29] It is the confidence to act in spite of the constantly threatening and enervating possibility that one's act may be futile and self-destructive. Accordingly, the courage of spiritual self-affirmation is the confidence that my use of reason to grasp and shape the world is a meaningful and significant use. When a man is estranged, however, this confidence is gone.[30] Given the discussion of estrangement as "unbelief," this turns out to be a tautology. It follows analytically that if, as happens in estrangement, a man loses an immediate awareness of the absolutes in his rational acts, then he loses confidence (i.e. certainty) that in his judgments he has purchase on the absolute standards of the true, the good, and the beautiful. If to have this confidence is to have the courage of spiritual self-affirmation, it follows that to be aware of the depth of reason (the unconditioned absolutes) is to have the courage to be.

Tillich's discussion of the modes of self-affirmation seems to make spiritual self-affirmation both the basis of anxiety about guilt and death and the basis of moral and ontic self-affirmation. He thereby

29. Ibid., pp. 162, 163, 164, 168.
30. Ibid., p. 48.

makes the ontological health of the total self dependent on the confidence ingredient in the proper use of reason. In the ontologically healthy man, anxiety is balanced by courage. However, the anxieties of guilt and death themselves presuppose the courage to affirm oneself spiritually. In the anxiety of guilt, even in its most extreme form, "doubt has not undermined the certainty of an ultimate responsibility."[31] The notion of "responsibility" is itself still meaningful. If, however, one loses the courage to affirm oneself spiritually and meaninglessness prevails, then even the certainty of an unconditional moral responsibility becomes doubted. In that case, it is impossible even to be anxious about guilt, for guilt itself has become a meaningless notion. So too, the anxiety of death at least presupposes the validity of the purposes and plans about whose successful actualization one is anxious. If there is no courage to affirm oneself spiritually and meaninglessness prevails, then the certainty of this presupposition goes and with it goes the very force of the anxiety. The necessary condition for feeling the anxiety of guilt or of death is the courage exercised in spiritual self-affirmation. The courage for spiritual self-affirmation is the minimum condition for being a self.

Furthermore, the courage of spiritual self-affirmation is the necessary condition for moral and ontic self-affirmation. To have the courage to affirm oneself morally is to have confidence in the validity of one's apprehension of "the moral norm," which, if obeyed, will preserve one's essential structure. It depends on having an awareness of the presence in one's life of "the unconditional element in the moral imperative" (*ST, 1,* 207). If man loses this awareness, then so far as the moral aspect of his human "being" is concerned he

31. Ibid., p. 174.

falls into the despair of having lost his destiny.[32] So too, the courage to affirm himself ontically presupposes the courage to affirm himself spiritually. Ontic courage consists in "vital strength." According to Tillich, the extent of a man's "vitality" is directly proportional to his "intentionality" (man's relation to "meaning"). Vitality, or the power of biological life, in man is intrinsically different from life power in other organisms precisely because it is the power of life that has conscious "relation to meanings."[33] But man is in fact related to meanings only by a use of reason in which the unconditioned absolutes effectively function. In this indirect way, man's vitality, and hence his courage to affirm himself ontically, depends on his courage to affirm himself spiritually. Since ontological health depends on having the courage to affirm oneself in all three aspects of human reality, it clearly depends on that proper use of reason that gives the courage of spiritual self-affirmation.

The Uses of Ontology

Tillich's discussions of the ontology of the self both in the *Systematic Theology* and in *The Courage To Be* entail three judgments. (1) The ontological well-being of the self depends on awareness of the presence of unconditioned absolutes in the use of reason. (2) Loss of awareness of this depth of reason results in ontological disruption of the self. (3) Having this awareness is essential to distinctively "human" being and its loss is an existential disruption of the self. These judgments can be used at a secondary level in theological arguments to warrant some of the generalizations about

32. Ibid., p. 52.
33. Ibid., pp. 78–81.

revelatory occurrences which in turn warrant, at a primary level of argument, theological conclusions about the biblical picture of Jesus as the Christ.

First, these judgments about the ontology of the self may be used to warrant the claim that revelatory occurrences are ontologically healing. The descriptive account of the dynamics of revelation showed that in revelatory occurrences a religious symbol or holy object evokes an odd discernment that the unconditioned power of being is in fact in one's life. The claim that this discernment is healing is warranted by ontological analysis, which shows that the health of the self depends on its having the awareness brought by this discernment. In the state of estrangement, the self is subjected to a process of ontological self-destruction precisely because it has lost this awareness. It needs to have restored to it an awareness of the presence of that which transcends the bounds of finitude. Since the phenomenological account of revelation showed that what is discerned in the revelatory event is precisely the fact that the unconditioned (depth of reason) *is* effectively present in one's life, the theologian is warranted in claiming that this discernment is ontologically healing.

Second, judgments about the ontology of the self may be used to warrant the claim that a revelatory occurrence always involves a receptive religious experience as well as a giving side. The theological conclusion is drawn that religious experience is a necessary condition for the occurrence of revelation but does not produce the occurrence or contribute to what it "manifests." Now, ontological analysis can show the following: (a) Religious experience is simply the essential possibility or a priori condition of coming to awareness of the presence of unconditional elements in one's rational activity.

(b) Regardless of whether religious experience can be self-generated, awareness of the depth of reason is not spontaneously actualized by men. (c) Any finite entity can serve to elicit discernment of man's continuing relatedness to the unconditioned. Tillich tries to make this third point by extending his analysis of distinctively "human" being to other sorts of being. He contends that, just as "human" being exhibits unconditional elements whose presence cannot be explained by reference to any features of finite human "being," so too all finite entities exhibit unconditional elements. At least they all exhibit the presence of a power by which they resist threats to their continuing existence. The presence of this power cannot be explained by reference to any qualities that characterize finite entities. This might be called the "self-transcendingness" of things; i.e. their character of including as a constituent element that which they do not produce, cannot "explain," and which must therefore be considered "transcendent" of them.[34] These ontological judgments may be used to warrant the claim that the necessary conditions for a revelatory occurrence are, on the receiving side, the religious a priori, or capacity for religious experience; and, on the giving side, a concrete holy object.

Both of these uses of ontological analysis lie at the level of secondary argument in which the move from backing to warrant at the first level of argument is defended. At the level of secondary argument, the data is what counts as backing at the primary level of argument. It consists of descriptive accounts of revelatory events stated in straightforward fact-claims. We noted in an earlier chapter that the normative instance of a revelatory event is the original

34. Cf. Tillich, *Dynamics of Faith*, p. 17; *ST*, 2, 7; *3*, 141; *Protestant Era*, p. 76.

Christian revelation as expressed in the biblical picture of Jesus as the Christ. It follows that, insofar as the picture is used as backing in theological argument, its use is directly controlled by ontological judgments, for ontology provides the warrants for such use. This is quite different from the use of the picture as normative data for theological argument. That use of the picture is not directly controlled by Tillich's ontology because the warrants licensing judgments come from analysis of revelations and not from ontology.

There is a third, rather different way in which ontology is used in theology. Ontological analysis yields terms which can also be used in religious discourse as religious symbols. "Spirit," "Logos," and "Being-itself" are examples. Used in ontological analysis, they are technical terms. Used in theology, they have a quite different logical status which Tillich usually designates "symbolic." Tillich characteristically distinguishes between the use of a term as a concept and the use of the same term as a religious symbol. He does this most extensively in a passage where he traces the history of the key terms of several different metaphysical systems, arguing that they all began as religious symbols and were "transformed" into names for the most basic or most ultimate dimension of reality (*ST, 1*, 230–35).[35] These two uses of the same terms are logically quite distinct.

There are three things ontological analysis cannot do. It is unable to show why one finite entity does in fact become a holy object occasioning a saving discernment for man while some other finite entity does not. This is important because it means that ontological analysis cannot show what it is about a given holy object that causes it to function as it does for those who "receive" it in ecstasy. All

35. Cf. *ST, 3*, 63, 417.

ontological analysis can show is that if a particular finite object does come to be "received" by man as a holy object and evokes in him a suitably odd discernment, then it has been the occasion for revelation–salvation for him. With respect to the biblical picture of Jesus as the Christ, this means that ontological analysis cannot help us in discovering what it is about the picture qua "expression" of a revelatory occurrence that causes it to function effectively qua "occasion" of revelatory occurrences.

The second thing ontological analysis is unable to do is to show with respect to any particular alleged revelatory occurrence that it truly is the unconditioned power of being that has been mediated there. At most it can show that there is such a power, that any given finite entity could occasion discernment of the presence of that power, and that such discernment would be ontologically healing if it came. However, it seems unable to show in any particular case that what was discerned was in fact this power, or that if there *appeared* to be ontological healing it truly was ontological healing, or that it was effected by the discernment and not by something else. This is important because it means that ontological analysis can never conclusively show that a given occurrence that appears to be revelatory of the unconditioned truly is revelatory. Put another way, it means that ontological analysis can never conclusively show that what is immediately experienced as an independent act of giving by the unconditioned truly is that, and not a hallucination. At most, ontological analysis can show that such an event *could* occur and if it did occur it would have the features that revelatory experiences have. With respect to the biblical picture of Jesus as the Christ, this means that ontological analysis does not in any way "guarantee" the truth of any particular theological claim to the effect that the biblical picture did in fact at some particular time and place evoke the healing discernment. Ontology may be able to warrant the judgment that, if it did occur, biblical revelation is the final or normative revelatory event, but it is unable to demonstrate that such revelation has in fact occurred.

Thirdly, ontological analysis is unable to yield a descriptive account of that which is manifested in revelation. This follows from Tillich's own account of the limits of knowledge and the subject matter of ontology. He explicitly recognizes it when he says that ontology cannot yield a doctrine of God (*ST, 1,* 243). If he sometimes appears to use the results of ontological analysis to "describe" God, he has overstepped bounds he himself set.

In short, while ontological analysis plays an important role at a second level of theological argument, it provides no way of evaluating religious symbols. It gives no criteria by which to test their truth, no way to distinguish symbols expressive of religious experience from symbols expressive of the occurrence of a revelatory event, and no explanation why some symbols expressive of original revelatory events can then serve to occasion dependent revelatory events.

Ontology and God as Spirit

It will be useful, both to illustrate and to test these points, to examine how Tillich uses ontological analysis in his discussion of God as Spirit. Tillich tells us that "Spirit" is "the most embracing, direct and unrestricted symbol for the divine life" (*ST, 1,* 249). It becomes unmistakably clear in the last two parts of Tillich's theology that "Spirit" is indeed his central theological term. God is simply identified with the "divine Spirit" (*ST, 3,* 140). That which was incarnate in Jesus and made him the Christ is identified as the "divine Spirit"; it is flatly identified with "the Son" (*ST, 3,* 144, 147–48) in the essential Trinity. In one place, a series of partly expressed and partly suppressed equations, the Spirit is identified with love, grace, and the power of New Being (*ST, 3,* 274). "God *is* Spirit": this is the most exhaustive and unqualified symbolic utterance that can be made "about" God. Initially, "spirit" is a technical term in Tillich's ontology. Ontological analysis does not state the meaning of the religious term "Spirit," but in ontology "spirit" is used to designate one of the dimensions of life. Life is the most basic ontological category. It is used to designate not simply organically living things, but anything whatsoever that is an "actualization of being," i.e. a concrete, individual actualization of the power to resist threats to its continued reality by means of self-integration, self-creativity, and self-transcendence (*ST, 3,* 11–12). There are a number of dimensions of life, such as the "vegetable" in which self-relating, self-increasing, and self-continuing activity takes place without any self-awareness, and the "animal" in which they occur with self-awareness. "Spirit" is that dimension of life in which this self-aware activity is joined with "eros, passion, imagination" and with a "*logos*-structure," i.e. the capacity to select freely chosen goals and the capacity to understand symbol systems. In brief, "spirit" is used "to denote the unity of life-power and life in meanings, or in condensed form, the 'unity of power and meaning' " (*ST, 3,* 24).[36] Whenever one encounters something that acts in a way that unites power and meaning, it may be classified as an instance of life in the spiritual dimension.

36. Cf. ibid., *1,* 249.

In the context of religious discourse, the ontological term "spirit" may be used as a religious symbol. Tillich specifies very carefully the conditions under which it is appropriate to do so. "Spirit is used to express the revelatory experience of 'God present' " (*ST, 3,* 11). Since revelatory occurrences are also "saving" occurrences, a man may use "Spirit" to express his involvement in any event in which the power of being is mediated to him anew. "Theologically speaking, Spirit, love, and grace are one and the same reality in different aspects" (*ST, 3,* 274).[37] It is appropriate to use "Spirit" under these conditions because these are experiences in which power and meaning are united. In these occurrences man receives the power that enables him to affirm himself despite ever present threats of guilt and meaninglessness. This power comes by means of insights and symbols that give an otherwise fragmentary and chaotic world coherence and meaning. It produces "unambiguous" life, i.e. life freed of existential disruptions. Tillich devotes much of Part IV of his *Systematic Theology* ("Life and the Spirit") to showing how this works out in both individual and communal life.

When "Spirit" is used as a religious symbol, it is no longer an ontological term. It is used in a logically quite distinct "language game." Tillich notes this by insisting that when "Spirit" is used as a religious symbol, "it has *not* been used as an adjective from spirit with a small 's,' designating a dimension of life." Therefore, it cannot be said that Tillich uses ontological analysis of life in its spiritual dimension to yield a technical term to express what the traditional theological term "Holy Spirit" really means. He does not use ontological terms to "translate" theological terms. To be sure, a term

37. Cf. ibid., *3,* 140.

ordinarily used in the context of ontology is also used in the context of religious discourse according to rules appropriate to that order of discourse, partly because the two contexts in which the term is used are not wholly dissimilar. In both cases, the term is appropriately used in reference to action in which power and meaning are united. But power and meaning are used in different ways in these two contexts, for the power and meaning united in the divine Spirit are non-finite or infinite in character. The divine Spirit "transcends" the power and meaning that spatially and temporally limited men can muster both in its inexhaustible capacity to withstand all threats and in its freedom from existential disruptions.

Ontological analysis cannot deal with such transcendent and infinite power and meaning. The nearest Tillich gets to giving a direct account of the divine Spirit in ontological terms is to say that the Spiritual Presence is the "dimension of depth" (*ST*, *3*, 113). "It is the 'depth' of all cultural creations and places them in a vertical relation to their ultimate ground and aim" (*ST*, *3*, 158). In the life of the individual it is the depth of reason (*ST*, *3*, 117, 119, 126, 132). This confirms our earlier judgment that in man renewed awareness of the presence of the unconditioned is identical with a renewed awareness of the depth of reason. But Tillich immediately qualifies these claims by insisting that "dimension" is used here in an entirely symbolic way. We do not have a straightforward ontological account of yet another dimension of life, namely the "depth dimension."

(It may be noted in passing that in this discussion Tillich also compromises the status of ontological analysis by insisting that its use of "dimension" is not straightforward either, but is metaphorical. His point is, nevertheless, that ontological and religious uses of

"Spirit" are logically diverse because where one is metaphorical the other is symbolical [*ST*, *3*, 113–14]).

As we have observed before, the most that Tillich can do with ontological analysis is to show why human life is ontologically disrupted and to show what a renewal of the Spiritual Presence or the presence of the power of being would do to heal life. He does this at great length in an analysis of ambiguities of life and the ways they distort man's moral, cultural, and religious life and in a description of how the divine Spirit's presence restores, albeit in a fragmentary way, unambiguous life (*ST*, *3*, 30–107, 167–283). But ontology cannot be used to demonstrate that there is such transcendent power and meaning or that they have ever been present in human life. It cannot be used to discover how such terms as "divine Spirit" and "Spiritual Presence" ought to be used or what such terms really mean.

If we want to know more exactly what "power" and "meaning" and "divine Spirit" mean, we must turn to an analysis of the revelatory and saving events whose occurrences are properly expressed by "Spirit." The sort of power and meaning that are united in "Spirit" will be the power and meaning manifested there. This confirms our earlier judgment that the warrants for theological judgments about the meaning of Christian religious symbols are provided by analysis of revelatory events and not by ontology.

An event in which the power of New Being is mediated to a man suffering the ambiguities of life created by his ontological disruptions is an event in which power and meaning are united because it "answers" his "question of unambiguous life" (*ST*, *3*, 113). However, as we have already seen, it should not be supposed that this answer consists of information, nor is the question a request for information. It is, as Tillich expressly puts it, a quest for unambiguous life (*ST*, *3*, 107–11). "The Spiritual Presence is not that of a teacher but of a meaning-bearing *power* which grasps the human spirit in an ecstatic experience" (*ST*, *3*, 115; my italics) and ends the quest by producing unambiguous life. Since the Spiritual Presence is identical with the renewed presence of the power of being in ontologically disrupted man, we can understand how the event in which the divine Spirit becomes present is an event in which power is present. But what sort of "meaning" is involved in the phrase "meaning-bearing power"?

Tillich does not answer this question explicitly, but the way he writes about the effects of encounter with Spiritual Presence in revelatory events strongly suggests that the "meaning" it gives is a sense of coherence or purpose or worth to life. When the divine Spirit is present, the ambiguities in language caused by the "split between subject and object" are overcome in a mode of speaking that both expresses "the union of him who speaks with that of which he speaks"[38] and unites "the centers of the speaker and the listener in the transcendent unity. Where there is Spirit, there estrangement, in terms of language, is overcome." Ambiguities in cognition are overcome "to the degree in which the subject–object structure is overcome" and "observation is replaced by participation . . . and conclusion is replaced by insight." Ambiguities in the self created by a split between the self as subject and the self as object are overcome when "the Spiritual Presence takes hold of a centered person," because "it re-establishes his identity unambiguously." Ambiguities in interpersonal relations are overcome under the same circumstances, for by mutual participation in a power that transcends

38. For what follows, see ibid., p. 253.

them both the self can relate to another who is "a stranger only in disguise" and is actually "an estranged part of one's self. Therefore one's own humanity can be realized only in reunion with him—a reunion which is also decisive for the realization of his humanity." Tillich also gives extended descriptions of how the Spiritual Presence overcomes a host of ambiguities in the religious, moral, and cultural aspects of communal life. The recurrent theme is that the divine Spirit reconciles broken human relations, creates coherent patterns in the jumble of men's ends and means, invests ordinary tools and daily labor with significance, and removes the demonic aspects of organized religion and the exercise of political power, thereby eliminating their inner contradictions. The divine Spirit gives meaning in an "axiological" sense of "meaning." It invests life with a felt-sense of its worth, of its significance and orderliness. It is in this sense that it is a "meaning-bearing power."

At every point of Tillich's exposition of the religious symbol "Spirit" our contentions have been supported. The warrants for judgments about the symbol are provided by analysis of revelatory events and not by ontology. At most, ontological analysis provides the warrants for a second-level argument designed to show that descriptive acounts of revelations do support generalized claims about how such events are healing as well as revealing. The fact that "Spirit" is a technical term in ontology does not mean that ontology gives the meaning of "Spirit" as a religious symbol.

4

HISTORICAL RESEARCH AND THEOLOGY

The theologian's task is to explicate the "content" of religious symbols found chiefly in the Bible. In what ways can historical investigations of the Bible contribute to this explication of the Christian message? It will be useful to break this question into two parts. What does historical criticism of the biblical texts and their history contribute to theology? And, what does investigation into the historical accuracy of biblical narratives contribute to Christian theology?

Tillich's general thesis is that, negatively, "historical research can neither give nor take away the foundation of the Christian faith" and that, positively, "historical research has influenced and must influence Christian theology" (*ST, 2,* 113).

The History of the Symbols

When Tillich specifies just how historical research must influence theology, he confines himself to a discussion of historical criticism of biblical texts and their history. He says such research helps theology three ways:

by giving an analysis of the three different semantic levels of biblical literature . . . ; second, by showing in several steps the development of the christological symbols . . . ; and, finally, by providing a precise philological and historical understanding of the biblical literature by means of the best methods developed in all historical work. (*ST, 2,* 113)

In three different ways, historical research can show something about what the verbal biblical symbols are and how they got that way. We shall want to know how such information helps the task of explicating their content.

Tillich's account of the three semantic levels of biblical literature is compressed into so short a paragraph that it is very difficult to know what he means. He clearly is distinguishing three modes of biblical narrative—"the empirically historical, the legendary, and the mythological" (*ST, 2,* 108). From the way Tillich discusses each of them, it appears that they differ in the extent to which historical fact-claims are made when each is used. Fact-claims about history are necessarily a part of what is said when the "empirically historical" form of narrative is used. Tillich says that the "legendary" form of expression "emphasizes the universal quality of particular stories" (*ST, 2,* 151) but does not explain what the "legendary" form is. In any case, he almost never uses it. The most important form of narrative by far is the "mythological," which is identical with the "symbolic." "Myths are symbols of faith combined in stories about divine-human encounters."[1] A claim about matters of historical fact is not part of what is said by the use of myths. As religious symbols, they are the way in which men express their participation in revelatory events and are not a way of referring to agents interacting through time. Since it is the central Christian religious symbol, the picture of Jesus as the Christ is stated at the mythological "semantic

1. Tillich, *Dynamics of Faith,* p. 49.

level." Theologically important content of the picture does not include historical fact-claims. The question of the historical accuracy of the narratives that together constitute the picture is theologically irrelevant, but this does not tell us positively what is the theologically significant content of the picture.

Secondly, historical research has shown that religious symbols develop in four steps. First, they arise in a given religious culture and language. Then they are used by succeeding generations to express their own existential situation and to express their answers to that situation. Third, they are appropriated by Christians as part of their symbolic expression of the original Christian revelatory event. Finally, they are distorted by popular superstition. Tillich is able to use this analysis to point up contrasts between the way symbols are used in Christian and in pre-Christian contexts. On the premise that the meaning of a symbol is determined by its use, this throws some light on the meaning of biblical religious symbols.

The third thing historical research does is to give increasingly reliable readings of the extant biblical texts. Since it is necessary to know what the biblical narrative symbols are before discussing what they mean, the relevance of this is obvious. Generally speaking, then, historical research can show just what the religious symbols in the Bible are and how they are used. The one positive claim is that Scripture is theologically significant precisely when its historical accuracy is least important, i.e. when it is construed as "mythological."

The Historicity of Jesus

Tillich's other claim is that "historical research can neither give nor take away the foundation of the Christian faith." Let us consider first the claim that historical research cannot take away the basis of Christian faith.

According to Tillich, the foundation of Christian faith is "Jesus as the Christ."[2] He makes some very emphatic statements to the effect that the historical reality of Jesus of Nazareth is an essential element in this foundation.

> The event on which Christianity is based has two sides: the fact which is called "Jesus of Nazareth" and the reception of this fact by those who receive him as the Christ.
>
> . . .
>
> And Christian theology as a whole is undercut if one of them is completely ignored. If theology ignores the fact to which the name of Jesus of Nazareth points, it ignores the basic Christian assertion that Essential God-Manhood has appeared within existence and subjected itself to the conditions of existence without being conquered by them. (*ST, 2,* 97, 98)[3]

Similarly, he says that the narratives about the crucifixion and resurrection "must be both reality and symbol." The stories about the cross "probably point to an event that took place in the full light of historical observation" (*ST, 2,* 153). The resurrection stories also have a factual element as a "necessary implication," although the fact was doubtless "a mysterious experience of a few" (*ST, 2,* 153–55).

This insistence on the factual element in the foundation of Christian faith seems to contradict Tillich's dictum that historical research

2. Cf. *ST, 2,* 98.
3. Cf. ibid., p. 107.

cannot take anything away from the foundation of Christian faith. Surely the fact-claim referred to by the name "Jesus of Nazareth" is, at least in principle, the sort of claim that historical research can disconfirm. If it is an essential element in the foundation of faith, then to that extent the basis of faith seems vulnerable to the negative results of historical research.

Tillich is anxious to show that this is not the case. Faith cannot rest on a basis that is so unsure that tomorrow might bring positive historical disconfirmation of it (*ST, 2*, 113–14). Faith and theology must rest on a foundation that faith itself can guarantee (*ST, 2*, 107, 114). To make his case, Tillich seems to distinguish between two factual elements—the fact-claim made about the existence and life of Jesus of Nazareth, which is vulnerable to historical criticism, and the fact-claim made about the foundation of Christian faith, which is not open to historical criticism. Thus, it turns out that he is misleading when he says, "If theology ignores the fact to which the name of Jesus of Nazareth points, it ignores the basic Christian assertion." The fact *named* by Jesus of Nazareth turns out to be different from the fact *pointed to* by Jesus of Nazareth. At any rate, that is what Tillich seems to be saying when he makes the following moves.

First, he points out the skeptical results of research into the "historical Jesus." It has been impossible "to discover a minimum of reliable facts about the man Jesus of Nazareth" (*ST, 2*, 105).[4] Furthermore, it is logically possible that historical criticism may find grounds for coming to the judgment that the man Jesus of Nazareth never lived. Fact-claims about one named Jesus of Naza-

---

4. Cf. ibid., p. 114.

reth are open to skeptical historical conclusions. Faith itself certainly cannot guarantee their truth.

Tillich then turns to noting what factual element faith *can* guarantee:

> faith can guarantee *only its own foundation,* namely, the appearance of that reality which has created the faith. This reality is the New Being, who conquers existential estrangement and thereby makes faith possible.

Thus far, it seems that the factual element in the foundation of faith is simply the fact that, for the man of faith, the power of being is newly present in his life. Tillich goes on to point out that faith can guarantee this fact analytically. Since faith is the state of the subject who has received the power of New Being, the judgment that a man has faith analytically entails the judgment that the power of New Being is present in him.

But then Tillich goes on to say that faith "guarantees *a personal life* in which the New Being has conquered the old being" *(ST, 2,* 113–14; my italics). The warrant for this judgment is not provided by historical research. Instead, it seems to be provided by analysis of the dynamics of revelatory events. Faith is the receiving act in a revelatory event; something objective and finite has to be the giving side. If a man has faith, it follows analytically that he is correlated in a revelatory constellation with some holy object. On the strength of the analysis of revelatory occurrences faith can guarantee that much.

But why does the holy object have to be "personal"? Tillich seems to support that elsewhere by appealing to his ontological analysis. The power of being could not have been manifested to men in any other way:

> for the potentialities of being are completely actual in personal life alone. . . . Only a person has . . . the structure of rationality. . . . Only a person has . . . finite freedom. Of no other being can all this be said. And only in such a being can the New Being appear. Only where existence is most radically existence—in him who is finite freedom—can existence be conquered. (*ST*, 2, 120)

The factual element that is a part of the foundation of faith is the fact that the power of being was mediated anew to the first disciples through a person. This is a fact faith can guarantee itself, given the results of analysis of revelation as warrant and the results of ontological analysis as backing. We cannot guarantee that the person through whom the power of being was mediated was named Jesus of Nazareth,[5] but stories about Jesus of Nazareth may be used to express or point to the fact that the power of being was once mediated through *somebody*. "Whatever his name, the New Being was and is actual in this man" (*ST*, 2, 114). It is in this way that historical research, while it may raise insuperable doubts about the existence and life of somebody named Jesus of Nazareth, cannot take away anything from the foundation of faith.

Tillich uses precisely the same distinction to argue for the certainty of the factual element in the accounts of the crucifixion and resurrection. Faith guarantees both. What is theologically important in the crucifixion is not the historical fact-claim that somebody

5. Cf. ibid., pp. 107, 114.

named Jesus was crucified. Rather, the immediate certainty of faith "is the surrender of him who is called the Christ to the ultimate consequences of existence, namely, death."[6] Faith guarantees that the holy object that was the giving side of original revelation was utterly self-negating. This is analytically true. Faith is the subjective state of one to whom the power of being has successfully been mediated. A holy object is unsuccessful in mediating this power if it draws attention to itself instead of to the power of being. The judgment that a man was in faith entails the judgment that the holy object that mediated the power of being to him did not draw attention to itself but instead "negated" itself. So too, the fact that faith guarantees in the resurrection stories is not the claim that a man named Jesus rose from the dead. Rather, the theologically important certainty is that "of one's own victory over the death of existential estrangement." It is tautological to say that faith is by definition the state of one to whom the power of being has been mediated so as to heal existential estrangement.

The Historical Accuracy of the "Analogy"

Is it impossible for historical research to add anything to the foundation of Christian faith? The basis of the faith of modern Christians has to be the biblical picture of Jesus as the Christ. Tillich contends that there is an *analogia imaginis* "between the picture and the actual personal life from which it has arisen." Could not historical research demonstrate that the picture does in fact accord well with that personal life? Tillich thinks the skeptical results of historical research in this area show that this is impossible.

6. For what follows, cf. ibid., p. 155.

Nevertheless, he launches into his own attempt to show that the picture is in fact analogous to its subject. Faith can "guarantee the biblical picture of Jesus as the Christ." It cannot guarantee its "empirical factuality," but it can guarantee that the picture is "an adequate expression of the transforming power of the New Being in Jesus as the Christ." Once again, the guarantee consists in a tautology. Christian faith is the state of a man to whom the power of being has been mediated anew through the biblical picture. Hence, the judgment that a man has faith entails the judgment that the picture is adequate as a mediator of the power of New Being.

Tillich concludes from this that there is an analogy between the picture and the one through whom the power of New Being was mediated to the first disciples:

> No special trait of this picture can be verified with certainty. But it can be definitely asserted that through this picture the New Being has power to transform those who are transformed by it. This implies that there is an *analogia imaginis,* namely, an analogy between the picture and the actual personal life from which it has arisen. (*ST, 2,* 114–15)

The analogy is implied by the fact that the picture fulfills a function in contemporary, dependent Christian revelations that is analogous to the function fulfilled by that anonymous "personal life" in the original Christian revelation: both mediate the power of New Being. The picture is analogous to its subject, but not because its details correspond in any way with what "actually happened." The analogy is purely one of function in revelatory occurrences. The clear implication is that the historical accuracy of the biblical picture is a matter of complete indifference to theology.

It is very odd, then, that a great deal of Tillich's discussion of Christology consists in arguments that are, at least covertly, designed to show that the biblical picture of Jesus as the Christ does correspond with historical fact. Scripture pictures a Jesus who was worthy of being received as the Christ. Tillich seems to want to show that the original disciples were justified in receiving Jesus as the Christ because such reception was in fact appropriate to what he was. This leads him to try to show that Jesus really must have been like the one pictured in Scripture.

We have already seen how Tillich argues that the giving side of original Christian revelation must have been a person. Consequently, it *must have been* the case that this person who was the giving side of original revelation was the only perfectly healed man, ontologically speaking. "In him the healing quality is complete and unlimited" (*ST, 2,* 168). This is true because, even though he lived within the conditions of existence, "his being [had] the quality of the New Being *beyond the split of essential and existential being."* Indeed, it is this fact about his being "that makes him the Christ" (*ST, 2,* 121) i.e. "the manifestation of the New Being in time and space."

It is because of this that Jesus as the Christ is the answer to men's existential questions or, perhaps better, the conclusion of their quests. For, "if there were no personal life in which existential estrangement had been overcome, the New Being would have remained a *quest* and an expectation and would not be a reality in time and space" (*ST, 2,* 98; my italics).

This person was not only perfectly healed; he also mediated the power of the New Being within the community of estranged men. Consequently, it must have been the case that he suffered and died:

Only by taking suffering and death upon himself could Jesus be the Christ, because only in this way could he participate completely in existence and conquer every force of estrangement which tried to dissolve his unity with God.

The suffering of Jesus as the Christ is an expression of the New Being in him. (*ST, 2*, 123, 124)[7]

The justification of this claim is also given by appeal to ontology. If the power of the New Being is to come to men, then it must appear among men who in fact are estranged. Since "the horror of death" and "meaningless suffering" are the result of man's estrangement, they must be part of the context within which the power of New Being appears if it is to appear at all.

There is another reason why it must have been the case that Jesus suffered and died. Any finite object that mediates the power of being must be "completely transparent to the mystery he reveals." There can be no identification of the conditioned with the unconditional. The finite object is only the occasion for the mediation of the power of being and does not itself have any unusual intrinsic relation to that power. Hence, the finite object is not important in and of itself but is important as a means by which the power can be mediated. It must, therefore, have "the power of negating itself without losing itself." If Jesus was able to mediate the power of the New Being to the original disciples, as in fact he did, it must have been the case that he did

surrender his finitude—not only his life, but also his finite power and knowledge and perfection. . . . But in order to be able to

7. Cf. ibid., pp. 135–36.

> surrender himself completely he must possess himself completely. And only he can possess—and therefore surrender—himself completely who is united with the ground of his being and meaning without separation and disruption. (*ST, 1,* 133)

He must not only have suffered and died, but also have been without "unbelief."[8]

Only if his actions had satisfied these conditions could Jesus (if that is his name) have so "impressed" the original disciples. Because, but only because, he did fill those conditions, he was final revelation; that is, he filled those conditions so completely that he is "the criterion of every assumed or real revelation" (*ST, 2,* 135) and "is the *finis* or *telos* (intrinsic aim) of all of them" (*ST, 1,* 137). That Jesus did "impress" the disciples in this way cannot be doubted:

> If Jesus had not impressed himself as the Christ on his disciples and through them upon all following generations, the man who is called Jesus of Nazareth would perhaps be remembered as a historically and religiously important person . . . but not the final manifestation of the New Being itself. (*ST, 2,* 99)

And it is appropriate that they should have been "impressed," i.e. that they should have received him as the Christ, for in him the New Being was "actualized in a personal life."

This is an astonishing argument for Tillich to include in his *Systematic Theology*. On his own grounds it can have no theological significance because it concerns itself with making claims about a historical figure while theology is supposed to be concerned with explicating the meaning of religious symbols and myths. It is also

8. Cf. ibid., p. 126.

a bad argument because it seems to be a covert form of the quest for the "historical Jesus." Claims are made about this figure in the historical past: he must have been a person, ontologically whole, crucified, etc. Tillich has already pointed out that such quests are not very fruitful and in any case yield problematic results.

Moreover, this historical quest uses the most irrelevant criteria as far as historical arguments go—the findings of ontological analysis. In each case, the historical conclusion was reached by showing that it "must be so" on *ontological* grounds. Historical claims are made about revelatory events. The events are analyzed in ontological terms. Then the claims about the events are justified on ontological grounds, when what was needed was independent support on historical grounds.

Thus, the comparison of the biblical account of Jesus with a picture is self-defeating because it is used to make contradictory claims. On the one hand, it is used as a way of denying that historical fact-claims are part of the biblical picture's meaning. On the other hand, it is used as the basis for an argument about what "must have been" the nature of that personal life (pointed to by Jesus of Nazareth) of which the picture is a picture—and that *is* an argument making historical fact-claims, albeit on improper grounds.[9]

Some Interim Conclusions

If the analysis of Tillich's treatment of Scripture is accurate thus far, some things may be said about what is *not* the theologically

9. For a very similar critique of Tillich's treatment of the historical Jesus by a New Testament scholar, see D. Moody Smith, "The Historical Jesus in Paul Tillich's Christology," *Journal of Religion, 46*, Pt. 2 (January 1966), 131–48.

significant content of Scripture. Biblical narratives might be theologically significant in that they accurately report sequences of past events. It would then be possible to specify what the biblical writings express in total independence of those narratives. Careful textual criticism of the Bible done in the light of the history of ideas in the ancient world would become theologically significant because it could exhibit, in partial independence of the Bible, what the biblical authors were thinking. It need not be argued that the findings of historical research could be substituted for the biblical narratives, as though the former were somehow an improved version of the latter. The biblical materials have roles to play in the life of the Christian community that no other writings can fill. Nevertheless, the Scriptures are taken by this point of view to be authoritative for theology primarily as reports about a sequence of events ("salvation history") occurring in the past and about a set of opinions held in the past ("biblical theology"). Scripture is theologically important this way because contemporary theology has to express the same opinions and make the same fact-claims today. Tillich's rejection of this proposal seems consistent and thoroughgoing.

Tillich is so thoroughgoing about this that he even insists that none of the historical Jesus' own ethical, cosmological, or theological ideas have any theological significance for the Christian. The crucifixion is our protection against making an idol of Jesus. It made a clear distinction between the finite holy object and the power mediated through him.

For us this means that in following him we are liberated from the authority of everything finite in him, from his special traditions, from his individual piety, from his rather conditioned world view, from any legalistic understanding of his ethics. (*ST, 1,* 134)

None of these elements (tradition, piety, world-view, ethics) is the theologically significant content of Scripture, even if it is an accurate account of what Jesus taught.

In Chapter 3 it was argued that Tillich does not in fact operate on the assumption that biblical writings are theologically important only insofar as they express certain highly general features of experience. If they were, it would be possible to specify what the writings express by recourse to ontological analysis. Analysis of the ontological structures of experience and being could show, in total independence of the Scriptures, what pervasive metaphysical facts are expressed by the notions of sin ("estrangement"), salvation ("reconciliation"), God ("First Cause"), etc. It need not be argued that the metaphysical terms should be substituted for the biblical ones. The biblical material undoubtedly fills roles in the life of the Christian community that no other literature could fill. Nevertheless, Scripture would be taken by this point of view to be authoritative for theology primarily as an intuitive and poetic expression of metaphysical facts. It is theologically important because contemporary theology has to try to make those poetic insights vivid in the modern world and must do so in such a way that they do not overlook the metaphysical profundity of the insight. However, on occasion Tillich explicitly rejects such straightforward translation of religious terms into ontological ones.[10] The usual function of his ontological analysis is to provide backing for warrants that license moves in theological

10. E.g. cf., re "Sin," *ST, 2,* 46; re "Salvation," *2,* 175.

argument from the data of religious symbols to judgments about their content.

In addition to rejecting historical research and ontology as translations of Scripture, Tillich rejects a third possible proposal about the content of the Bible. It could be proposed that biblical narratives are theologically significant primarily as they express the private religious experience of the first disciples. Given this view, it would be possible to specify what the biblical writings express by giving phenomenological account of religious experience. It need not be argued that philosophy of religion could be substituted for the biblical narratives, as though it "said the same thing." Nevertheless, Scripture would be important if taken this way because contemporary theology, if it wishes to be Christian, must discuss present-day versions of the same experience. Tillich rejects this view. For him, religious symbols in Scripture are theologically significant primarily as they express, not the experience of receiving in a revelatory event, but the objective giving element in revelations. As seen in Chapter 2, the principal function of his own phenomenological account of religious experience and revelation is to provide warrants for moves in theological argument from the symbols as data to conclusions about their content.

5

THE CONTENT OF A VERBAL ICON

          Scripture provides the central data for Tillich's theological argument when biblical writings are construed as a single verbal icon, viz., the biblical picture of Jesus as the Christ. It is chiefly by providing this major datum that Scripture is authoritative for theology. The procedure Tillich uses to explicate the content of Scripture is analogous to the procedure used to explicate any icon. It is an act of "criticism" based on certain aesthetic principles, which is to say that aesthetics provides warrants for judgments made about the picture.

    It turns out that Tillich actually employs two quite different procedures in explicating the content of the biblical picture, and they seem to be warranted by two quite different aesthetics. One of these supposes that the content of the picture lies somehow outside the picture itself and that criticism consists in drawing the beholder's attention to this content. (This will be examined in the next chapter.) The other supposes that the content of the picture consists in its formal properties. It supposes an aesthetic that identifies the "meaning" of a work of art with its form. In the case of the biblical picture of Jesus as the Christ, this consists in the pattern of relationships that obtains among the symbols which are component parts of the picture.

Showing how symbols in a set are related to one another and to the whole to which they belong is the theological task of "conceptualizing." A great deal of Tillich's discussion of Christology consists in doing just this. It is important for him to do so because it is his way of establishing the continuity between the content of the Christian message as he understands it and the content of original Christian revelation. The picture guarantees this continuity. Original revelation occurred when the disciples met Jesus and received the power of being mediated through him. The picture of Jesus as the Christ is their "creative response" (*ST, 1,* 35)[1] to this encounter. The picture is somehow appropriate or responsible to its subject. There is "an *analogia imaginis* . . . an analogy between the picture and the actual personal life from which it has arisen" (*ST, 2,* 115).[2] The picture then serves as the giving side of dependent revelatory occurrences. Its analogy with the giving side of original revelation assures a continuity of content between the original and dependent revelatory events. It is because of the picture that the New Testament, the "original document" (*ST, 2,* 117)[3] on which church theology has always been based, has been authoritative for theology.

As we have seen, the proposal that scriptural narratives bear *analogia imaginis* to their subject is a way of outflanking the problems raised by the historical unreliability of the stories. Tillich introduces the idea of the analogy in a passage where he argues that "historical research can neither give nor take away the foundation

1. Cf. *ST, 2,* 115.
2. Cf. ibid., *1,* 126.
3. Cf. ibid., *2,* 115.

of the Christian faith." The biblical picture is the foundation of faith for men in dependent revelation, and it is theologically significant only insofar as it functions in this way. Apparently its ability to do this is not dependent on its historical accuracy. Instead, Tillich's considerable attention to the picture's formal properties suggests that somehow they enable it to fill the role of miracle in dependent Christian revelation.

The Picture as Verbal Icon

The biblical picture of Jesus as the Christ is, like any icon, a work of the imagination. Tillich himself underscores this point. He contends that it is a picture in the same sense that a portrait in the expressionist style is a picture:

> In this approach a painter would try to enter into the deepest levels of the person with whom he deals. And he could do so only by a profound participation in the reality and meaning of his subject matter. Only then could he paint this person in such a way that his surface traits are neither reproduced as in photography (or naturalistically imitated) nor idealized according to the painter's ideal of beauty but are used to express what the painter has experienced through his participation in the being of his subject. This third way is meant when we use the term "real picture" with reference to the Gospel records of Jesus as the Christ. (*ST, 2,* 116)

Like a portrait, it does have a subject who existed and was independent of the picture. The biblical picture does not bear a point-for-point correspondence with its subject; this would be a picture in the photographic style. Nor is it the product of a freewheeling imagination, a "painted projection of the experiences and ideals of the most religiously profound minds in the period of the Emperor Augustus." Such a painting would be in the idealistic style and would have no real subject other than the psyche of the man creating the picture. However, the biblical picture does have a subject other than the ideals and aspirations of the men who created it, and it is somehow appropriate to its subject. The appropriateness is analogical.

The biblical picture is like other works of the imagination in another respect. It is "absolutely concrete and absolutely universal at the same time." Tillich contends that the giving side of any revelatory event has to have these properties. How is it possible for one thing to be both absolutely concrete and absolutely universal? In the first place, "universal" must be distinguished from "abstract" and "concrete" from "particular." It is impossible to be both abstract and particular. Both are what they are by excluding something else. "Abstraction negates parts of that from which it abstracts," and "particularity excludes every particular from every other one." Hence,

> Something that is merely abstract has a limited universality because it is restricted to the realities from which it is abstracted. Something merely particular has a limited concreteness because it must exclude other particular realities in order to maintain itself as concrete. Only that which has the power of *representing* everything particular is absolutely concrete. And only that which has the power of *representing* everything abstract is absolutely universal. (*ST, 1,* 16; my italics)[4]

4. Cf. ibid., p. 151.

According to Tillich, the "given" which the first disciples received in the occurrence of original Christian revelation did represent everything particular and everything abstract.

Similar claims are sometimes made about significant works of the imagination. They are utterly concrete in that they are highly specific and detailed in content and deliberate in form. They are uniquely what they are and are not simply interchangeable instances of some more general type. At the same time, they must be universal if they are at all significant. They must exhibit some feature of our common human life, express or evoke some experience that is widely shared, or offer some perspective on the world that others besides the artist can be brought to share.

Some of the "new critics" have tried to explain this conjunction of concreteness and universality in works of literature in terms very like Tillich's. Thus, W. K. Wimsatt, Jr., writes:

A literary work of art is a complex of detail (an artifact, if we may be allowed that metaphor for what is only a verbal object), a composition so complicated of human values that its interpretation is dictated by the understanding of it, and so complicated as to seem in the highest degree individual—a concrete universal.

He then goes on to show how "metaphoric structure" in a variety of forms can make a poem at once concrete and universal by making it at once complex and unified.[5] It becomes a verbal icon. Allen Tate has argued that this characteristic of poetry is a function of a poem's "tension," i.e. "the full organized body of all the extension

5. W. K. Wimsatt, Jr., *The Verbal Icon* (New York, Noonday Press, 1958), pp. 77, 80–82.

and intension we can find in it." The "extension" of the terms is the range of individuals denoted by the terms; "intension" is the total of qualities connoted. Apparently, concreteness comes from the former and universality from the latter.

> The metaphysical poet as a rationalist begins at or near the extensive or denoting end of the line; the romantic or Symbolist poet at the other, intensive end; and each by a straining feat of the imagination tries to push his meanings as far as he can toward the opposite end, so as to occupy the entire scale.[6]

By this more technical terminology, Tate also seems to be claiming that the concrete–universal characteristic of works of the imagination is a function of their formal properties.

The way Tillich compares the verbal biblical picture of Jesus as the Christ with painting suggests that it is a verbal icon. As the giving side of dependent revelation, the picture would have to be both concrete and universal. Tillich seems to want to say that it has both of these characteristics for the same reason that poems have them, viz., because of certain formal features.

The biblical picture, like any good work of the imagination, is very concrete:

> The biblical picture of Jesus is that of a unique event. Jesus appears as an individual beside others, but unique in his destiny, in every single trait of his character, and in his historical setting. It was just this concreteness and incomparable uniqueness of the "real" picture which gave Christianity its superiority over mystery

6. Tate, *Man of Letters*, pp. 71, 74.

cults and Gnostic visions. A real, individual life shines through all his utterances and actions. In comparison, the divine figures of the mystery cults remain abstract, without the fresh colors of a life really lived and without historical destiny and the tensions of finite freedom. The picture of Jesus as the Christ conquered them through the power of a concrete reality. (*ST*, 2, 151)

The picture is concrete because it successfully renders a believable individual character and not some sort of abstract type of the class "humanity" or of the smaller class "spiritual men." Clearly, the picture does this through its "anecdotal" style. It renders a believable character by telling *stories* about "all his utterances and actions."

The narrative style of the biblical picture also gives the picture its universality. When Tillich points out that historical study of the development of Scripture has shown three different forms of semantic expression, he contends that each form gives the picture a different mode of universality. The empirically historical form of narrative expresses the narrative's value "in answering the questions of human existence generally," i.e. universally. The legendary form of expression "emphasizes the universal quality of particular stories," and the mythological form of narrative "expresses the universal meaning of the whole event of Jesus of Nazareth" (*ST*, 2, 151). Since Tillich fails to make clear precisely how these three forms of narrative are to be identified, the claim that they give the picture its universality has no clear meaning. Nevertheless, it clearly seems to be his intention to relate the way the picture functions in dependent revelations with its formal properties. It can function as the giving side of revelatory events because its formal properties as narrative make it at once concrete and universal: the picture is a verbal icon.

Tillich's proposal that Scripture is theologically significant only to the extent that it renders a verbal icon has an immediate attractiveness. It promises a way out of difficulties theologians meet in their effort to do theology "in accord with Scripture" when they acknowledge that scriptural historical accounts are of dubious accuracy. Unfortunately, the proposal has a serious flaw.

It is never shown that the biblical picture is specifically like expressionist portraits at all. The expressionist style, as Tillich himself has noted,[7] commonly involves exaggeration and distortion of the subject being painted. Rather than simply reproducing the subject's surface traits photographically or idealizing them, a portraitist painting in the expressionist style uses distortions of his subject's surface traits in order "to express what the painter has experienced through his participation in the being of his subject." What the painter has experienced is not so much his own reactions to his subject as the "deepest levels" of the subject, levels which are not empirically available.

Tillich seems to be saying that in a corresponding way the formal features of the verbal picture of Jesus as the Christ express Jesus' "deepest levels" and precisely thereby express his universality. Thus, when we "look" at the biblical picture,

> we can say that we know nobody as well as Jesus. In contrast to all other persons, the participation in him takes place not in the realm of contingent human individuality (which can never be approached completely by any other individual) but in the realm of his own participation in God, a participation which, in spite of the mystery of every person's relation to God, has a universality in

7. Tillich, *The Courage To Be,* p. 146.

which everyone can participate. Of course, in terms of historical documentation we do know many people better than Jesus. But in terms of personal participation in his being, we do not know anyone better because his being is the New Being which is universally valid for every human being. (*ST, 2,* 116)

This might be taken to mean that the formal features of the biblical picture reveal the deepest levels of Jesus, just as the formal features of expressionist painting reveal the deepest levels of its subjects. In this sense, one might claim to have been brought by the picture to "know" the person in a more thoroughgoing way, to understand him more fully, etc. This might be what is meant by saying that the picture makes it possible for everyone to "participate" in him.

However, it would be difficult to show that the style of the Synoptic Gospels' stories involves this sort of exaggeration and distortion of Jesus' surface traits. Indeed, it would be hard to show that the biblical picture tries at all to express the deepest levels, the agonies, profundities of suffering, heights of sensitivity, etc. of Jesus. On the contrary, as Tillich himself expressly points out, the New Testament writers are not interested in expressing Jesus' "inner life." Jesus' individual character, which is precisely what expressionist painting would attempt to express, is virtually eliminated in the picture (*ST, 2,* 151).[8] The biblical material itself, then, does not support the parallel Tillich has drawn with expressionist painting. It is far from clear what light has been thrown on the theological content of Scripture by construing in terms of this model. If the biblical picture is not in the expressionist style, so that its very inaccuracies are what make it appropriate to its subject, what kind of a picture is it?

8. Cf. *ST, 2,* 116.

Formal Analysis of the Picture

Regardless of the answer to this question, it is clear that Tillich spends a great deal of time explicating the content of the picture by exhibiting its formal structure. His very procedure suggests that the analogy the picture has with its subject lies in the picture's inner structure. This too, unfortunately, turns out to be misleading.

According to Tillich's analysis, the picture is organized about two central component symbols, the "Cross of the Christ" and the "Resurrection of the Christ." These two symbols

> correspond to the two basic relations of the Christ to existential estrangement. . . . The first relation of the Christ to existence is his subjection to it; the second relation of the Christ is his conquest of it. All other relations are directly or indirectly dependent on these two. Each of them is expressed by a central symbol. The subjection to existence is expressed by the symbol of the "Cross of the Christ"; the conquest of existence is expressed in the symbol of the "Resurrection of the Christ." (*ST, 2*, 152–53)

As is characteristic of biblical symbols, both Cross of the Christ and Resurrection of the Christ consist of stories. Both sets of stories are about Jesus *as the Christ;* that is, both sets of stories have a protagonist who is the one "who brings the new state of things, the New Being" *(ST, 2*, 99). The set of stories constituting the Cross of the Christ symbol and the set constituting the Resurrection of the Christ symbol each have what Tillich calls "corroborating" symbols. These also consist in narratives and are interpreted by showing their relation to one or the other or both of the central symbols. Tillich seems to take the central symbols to be expressive of the giving side of original Christian revelation. Furthermore, the way he talks about them suggests that in his view they primarily express the way in which that giving took place.

The Cross of the Christ is the symbolic expression of "the subjection of him in whom the New Being is present by the conditions of existential estrangement."[9] "Cross" expresses something about the way in which the power of being was mediated anew in original Christian revelation: the act of giving took place within the context of existential estrangement and even took place through one who fully participated in that situation. Men did not have to remove themselves from their existential predicament before the power of being could once again be immediately present in their lives. Rather, the power of being became present once again in their lives right in the midst of their estranged condition.

There are other symbols in the New Testament that corroborate this one. Tillich holds that Paul is expressing the same feature of the giving side of original Christian revelation when, in the second chapter of Philippians, he tells the story of how the preexistent Christ surrendered his divine form to become a servant and experience death as a slave. Such a narrative about an encounter of God with man is a "myth." It cannot be taken literally as an account of "an event which happened at some time in the heavenly place." Rather, it expresses one aspect of the way in which the power of being was mediated to men in original Christian revelation. Tillich also classifies the stories of Christ's birth, his flight to Egypt, and the early threat to his life by political powers as symbols corroborating the symbol of the cross. So are all the stories about Jesus' subjection to

9. For what follows, see ibid., pp. 155–60.

finitude and its estrangement, for example, the stories about the agony in Gethsemane. These stories

> are not important in themselves in the context of the biblical picture. They are important in their power to show the subjection of him who is the bearer of the New Being to the destructive structures of the old being.

Thereby they express one aspect of the giving side of original Christian revelation.

The Resurrection of the Christ is the symbolic expression of "the victory of Christ over the ultimate consequences of existential estrangement to which he subjected himself." "Resurrection" also expresses something about the way in which the power of being was mediated anew in original Christian revelation: the act of giving has made "real" and a matter of immediate experience man's unity with the power of being. Man does not have to remain in the state of existential estrangement from the power of being in order to be a man.

There are other symbols in the New Testament that corroborate this one. Stories about the preexistence of the Son of God express "the eternal root of the New Being as it is historically present in the event of Jesus as the Christ." Stories about his post-existence express the unity of this historical event with the power of being, unbroken even by Jesus' historical career. Although he thinks the virgin birth a misleading symbol, Tillich takes the stories about it to be expressing the same point in another way: the unbroken unity between holy object and power of being is expressed in stories about how "the divine Spirit who has made the man Jesus of Nazareth into the Messiah has already created him as his vessel, so that the saving

appearance of the New Being is independent of historical contin-
gencies and dependent on God alone." So too, the miracle stories
symbolically express the experience that "the saving power of the
New Being is, above all, power over the enslaving structures of evil."
Tillich takes the stories about the ascension and the second coming
to be expressive of the same aspect of the way in which the power
of being was mediated in original Christian revelation. All of these
stories are symbols expressing the experience of unbroken unity
with the power of being.

Both cross and resurrection seem to be symbols expressing two
different aspects of the way in which giving took place in original
Christian revelation. At any rate, it seems that these central symbols
are important for theology only insofar as they express the way in
which the giving took place. This stands in contrast with our initial
impression that the picture was analogous, not to the way something
happened, but to someone.

This reading of Tillich is further supported by his claim that the
two central symbols "cannot be *separated* without losing their meaning." The two sets of stories that comprise each of the central
symbols have the same protagonist. He is not Jesus of Nazareth
who was the subject or agent of a series of contingently related
episodes in past history, including a painful death and a rather odd
afterlife. Rather, he is Jesus qua the mediator of the power of New
Being, Jesus as the Christ. The two sets of stories express two
aspects of the way in which he functioned as mediator. Hence, the
stories are inseparable. The stories about one who is subjected to
the conditions of existence (Cross of the Christ) are nonetheless
stories about one who did mediate the power of being within those
conditions, i.e. exhibited unbroken unity with the power of being

(Resurrection of the Christ). If the story of the cross were separated from the story of the resurrection, then, says Tillich, it would merely be the story of "one more tragic event." Such a story might express man's continuing existential predicament, but it would not be the expression of an aspect of the giving side of a revelatory and heal-ing act. So too, the stories about one who "conquers" the conditions of existence (Resurrection of the Christ) are nonetheless stories about one who had this unity with the power of being precisely within the context of existential estrangement (Cross of the Christ). If the story of the resurrection were separated from the story of the cross, then, Tillich claims, it "would be only one more questionable miracle story" (*ST, 2*, 153). Such a story might express man's quest for escape from his existential predicament, but it would not be the expression of an aspect of the giving side of any revelatory and saving event that could occur *in* his life. Tillich defends the claim that the central symbols are inseparable by arguing that they express two inseparable aspects of the way in which the giving side of original Christian revelation occurred.

Tillich calls the juxtaposition of these two symbols "paradoxical." There is no logical incompatibility between a story telling about Jesus as a man subject to the conditions of existence and a story telling about Jesus as one who conquers the conditions of existence. However, telling both stories about one person runs contrary to re-ceived opinion about what can be expected of human life. That is precisely what constitutes a paradox, i.e. something that runs against "the opinion which is based on the whole of ordinary human ex-perience" (*ST, 2,* 92).

The paradoxical quality of the relation between the set of stories comprising the Cross of the Christ symbol and the set of stories comprising the Resurrection of the Christ symbol is the dominant *formal property* of the biblical picture of Jesus as the Christ. It is analogous, not so much to the person of Jesus, as to the dynamics of the giving side of original Christian revelation.

The tension between the two central symbols constituting the picture of Jesus as the Christ is the key to the theological significance of another set of symbols. Terms like "incarnation," "redemption," and "justification" themselves designate sets of religious symbols. They must be explicated in terms of their formal relations to the biblical picture. It turns out that each of them expresses both of the aspects of the revelatory event that are expressed, respectively, by crucifixion and resurrection narratives.

> There is, in the last analysis, only *one* genuine paradox in the Christian message—the appearance of that which conquers existence under the conditions of existence. Incarnation, redemption, justification, etc., are implied in this paradoxical event. (*ST, 1,* 57; my italics)

For example, the symbol "redemption" is made up of stories, e.g. how Jesus redeemed men from the power of death or the power of sin or, in patristic theology, the power of the devil. These stories express the saving event, but with particular emphasis on one consequence of the event—liberation from demonic, i.e. destructive, powers (*ST, 1,* 57).[10] Hence, these stories, and thereby the symbol "redemption," must be explicated so as to show how they express both aspects of the paradoxical way in which the giving side of the liberating event occurred.

10. Cf. ibid., p. 170.

Even the stories comprising the symbol "incarnation" express the occurrence of the saving event. This seems to be unlikely, since those stories appear to express something paradoxical about the person of Jesus (he was "God" as well as "man") rather than about his work. However, Tillich denies the validity of this distinction. The stories making up the symbol "incarnation" only concern Jesus as the Christ, i.e. they only concern Jesus insofar as he functions effectively to mediate the power of New Being. "Christology is a function of soteriology" (*ST, 2,* 150).[11] Consequently, christological stories, e.g. the stories comprising the symbol "incarnation," must be expressive of the paradoxical way in which the giving side of original revelation occurred.[12] More clearly, perhaps, than other narratives, these symbols are analogous to the dynamics of the giving side of original revelation rather than to the person of Jesus.

There is still another set of religious symbols that may have theological significance if they are related to the central Christian symbols "cross" and "resurrection." These are symbols that express the occurrence of revelatory events that are not dependent on the original Christian revelation. Nevertheless, they come to be related to the Christian revelation because they provide the necessary condition for the reception of Christian revelation by men who have never heard of it before. Without them "final revelation would not have been understandable," for "no categories and forms would exist to receive final revelation" (*ST, 1,* 139). Tillich calls them the symbols expressive of "preparatory revelation." Such revelation is universal in the sense that it is a "universal possibility." In this

11. Cf. ibid., p. 146.
12. For similar accounts of "regeneration," "sanctification," and "justification," see ibid., pp. 176–80.

connection, Tillich gives special attention to Old Testament religious symbols. His treatment of the symbol "Messiah" is a representative case, because it figures most prominently in Tillich's own theology in the ubiquitous phrase, "Jesus as the Christ" (where "Christ" is, of course, simply the Greek equivalent for "Messiah").[13]

The dominant formal feature of the pattern of relationship between symbols of preparatory revelation and the central symbols of Christian revelation is, again, paradox. Since preparatory symbols are a necessary condition of the intelligibility of Christian symbols, they must be "categories and forms" that are appropriate to the Christian message. Thus, Christians used the Jewish religious symbol "Messiah" to describe Jesus in order to make his significance intelligible to Jews.

Tillich exhibits the meaning of the symbol "Messiah" by summarizing a set of stories whose protagonist is regularly referred to as Messiah. The thing all the stories have in common is the function performed by their protagonist. He brings the ideal conditions for life by setting up his reign; in the broadest sense of the phrase, he brings the power of New Being. In all these stories, therefore, the term "Messiah" is "the symbolic designation of a function" (*ST, 2,* 111). The stories within the family differ in the ways in which they depict the protagonist performing his function. In every case, however, the function that needs to be performed is seen as performed in only one act that, once done, need never be repeated.

This suggests that Messiah is very nearly, but not quite, the same as a personal name. When we try to explain what the name Abraham Lincoln might "mean," we finally have to tell stories about him.

13. For similar treatments of "Son of Man," "Son of God," and "Logos," see ibid., pp. 109–13.

We can, to be sure, begin by locating him as an instance of various classes (e.g. he is a man, over six feet tall, Illinois-born, etc.), but this fails to show what sort of a person he was. We may then try comparing him with other men already familiar to our listener, but the comparisons will be vague until we begin to tell stories about him which will indicate more concretely just how he was like and how he was unlike other men. His uniqueness as a person requires telling stories about him in an effort to explain what (or rather, whom) the name Abraham Lincoln designates or "means." For precisely the same reason people have had to resort to story-telling to explain what "Messiah" means. The term designates a function which is, in its important characteristics, unique; it can be performed only once. Consequently, the character of the function cannot be adequately described by locating it as one instance of a class of performances of which other instances are already known. In this way, the term "Messiah" is very like a personal name.

However, it does designate a function and not a person. No person performs just one function. Therefore, a term designating just one function could not be taken to be the same as a personal name. This, I take it, is Tillich's point when he says that the symbol "Messiah" is distorted at a later step of its development precisely by being confused with a personal name and taken to be Jesus' surname. If this is so, then one can use Messiah to designate a function only if by Messiah one refers the reader (or hearer) to a whole family of stories by which the unique function can be specified. When Christians described Jesus as the Messiah, they were, in effect, tying this family of stories in with the set of stories constituting the central Christian religious symbols "cross" and "resurrection." This was a way of making the significance of the Christian symbols intelligible to people already familiar with the symbol "Messiah." This use of Messiah to explicate the content of Christian revelation seems to rest on the supposition that the preparatory symbol does not seriously distort that content.

At the same time it must be said that the original Christian revelatory occurrence shows that previous manifestations of the power of being are in need of correction, even if they are preparatory:

> It [the original Christian revelatory event] could not have occurred without having been expected, and it could not have been expected if it had not been preceded by other revelations which had *become distorted.* (*ST, 1,* 137; my italics)

Accordingly, the symbols expressing preparatory revelations, such as Messiah, need some sort of correction before they can be used to help express Christian revelation. The preparatory symbol may be used, but in a way contrary to received opinion about how it ought to be used. This paradox must be formally reflected in the very way in which Messiah, for example, and the central Christian symbols are related to one another within the biblical picture of Jesus as the Christ.

The biblical picture consists of stories about a defeated and crucified man. However, by using the symbol "Messiah" to help tell these stories, the biblical picture classifies its stories as members of the family of Messiah stories, all of which are about a powerful and victorious protagonist. The picture is justified in classifying its stories with Messiah stories because its stories tell in imaginative recollection about one who once and for all performed the unique function that Messiah stories tell about in imaginative hope. Nonetheless, with respect to the way in which its protagonist performs his function, the biblical picture does not belong with the other Messiah stories. On their ground, "defeated Messiah is not a Messiah at all" (*ST, 2,* 111). There is, in short, a tension within the biblical picture between its Messiah and cross component symbols, in which cross *seems* to negate Messiah but in fact simply makes Messiah more precise. In other words, the fact that the picture is a story about a defeated man *seems* to exclude its being a story about a victorious figure, but in fact only specifies with more precision just how the victorious figure performs the victorious function he is said to perform. This tension is the way in which the biblical picture corrects the component symbol that it uses. By juxtaposing in a paradox the component symbols "Messiah" and "cross," the picture at once classifies itself with Messiah stories, negates its status among Messiah stories, and specifies the unique way in which it is the final form of Messiah story. Once again, the formal structure of the picture is analogous, not to any features of the person Jesus, but to the dynamics of the giving side of original revelation.

When biblical literature is taken to be theologically significant only if construed analogously with a work of art, theological explication of its content will consist in an analysis of its formal features. The analysis exhibits the patterns in which sets of narratives have deliberately been juxtaposed to form a single picture of Jesus as the Christ. This is the way in which "conceptualization" is done on the picture, i.e. the way in which one shows how the sets of symbols comprising the picture as a whole are related to each other and to the whole to which they belong. The dominant feature of these relationships is the tension created by paradoxically holding together two stories that conventional wisdom considers contrary to one another. Because of this tension, the pattern in which the biblical narratives have been imaginatively brought together bears *analogia imaginis,* not to the person of Jesus, but to the way in which the original Christian revelation was given.

This means, however, that the original explanation of the notion of *analogia imaginis* was seriously misleading. The locus classicus says that it is an analogy "between the picture and the actual personal life from which it has arisen" (*ST, 2,* 115). This suggests that, in virtue of its formal features, the biblical picture is analogous to the individual personal character, if not of Jesus, then of someone traditionally "pointed to" by the name Jesus. It would be precisely such an appropriateness of the picture to its personal subject that would guarantee the continuity of dependent revelatory events, in which the picture is the giving side, with the original revelation, in which Jesus was the giving side. On this basis Tillich seemed justified in spending a good deal of his discussion of Christology in a description of the formal structure of the picture.[14] On Tillich's own grounds, that is the way to ensure that what is said today on the basis of Scripture ("using the picture as datum") is said in continuity with the content of the original Christian revelation.

However, it turns out that the biblical picture is really analogous, not to the important features of some personal life, but to the pattern of the way in which something happened through this personal life, viz., the mediation of the power of being to the original disciples. But if the subject of the picture is an event and not a personal life, it is

14. Roughly half of Tillich's discussion of substantive issues in Christology is spent in argument about what Jesus "must have been like" (ibid., pp. 118–38); this section was discussed in Chapter 4. The other half is devoted to description of the formal structure of the biblical picture of Jesus as the Christ or to explication of other notions *in terms of* that formal analysis (ibid., pp. 150–80).

not clear why theology need concern itself with Scripture as a portrait of a person. For the same reason it becomes unclear how attending to the formal features of the picture as a portrait can ensure a continuity of content between theology today and original Christian revelation. If the picture is the major datum for theology and its subject is not a person, it is hard to see how Christology or even distinctively Christian theology is possible.

6

THE CONTENT OF A HOLY OBJECT

The biblical picture of Jesus as the Christ is not only the symbolic expression of the occurrence of original revelation; it is also the miracle or holy object in dependent Christian revelations. While Tillich's explication of the picture as expressive symbol suggests that its content is its form, his explication of it as holy object suggests that its content is something quite different and, unfortunately, quite unrelated. What makes it the central Christian religious symbol is its formal analogy with the miracle element in the original Christian revelation, but what makes it the central religious symbol for Christian theology *today* is its functional analogy with the miracle element in original revelation. It too mediates the power of being and that power is its significant content. Criticism of the picture, i.e. distinguishing it from other valid, less valid, and invalid religious symbols, consists in assessing how well it does this job. This sort of explication of the picture seems to be warranted by an aesthetic that finds the content of a work of art to be outside the picture itself, either in the emotional experience the artist intends to express or in the experience the work evokes in the beholder. Tillich's failure to show any connection between these two senses in which the picture has content leaves an important structural flaw in his systematic theology.

Power as Content

The biblical picture of Jesus as the Christ is of central importance to the church theologian today because "it was this picture which created both the church and the Christian. . . . But the picture has this creative power because the power of the New Being is expressed in and through it" (*ST, 2,* 115). The picture serves as the miracle element in dependent Christian revelations. As seen in Tillich's analysis of the dynamics of revelatory events, what is manifested through a holy object is not information but simply the effective presence of the power of New Being. The content of the picture is power.

Tillich relies on this formula when he tries to show that, despite its inner complexity and apparent inconsistencies, the New Testament's account of Jesus has an underlying unity. He notes that, while the synoptic Gospels emphasize "the participation of the New Being in the conditions of existence," the Johannine interpretation emphasizes "the victory of the New Being over the conditions of existence." These two cannot be combined to produce a harmonious historical picture. So too, there is a serious systematic problem created by the contrast between the "kingdom-centered sayings of Jesus in the Synoptics and the Christ-centered nature of his sayings in John." Furthermore, there is considerable diversity in the sorts of "eschatological framework" in which Jesus is reported to have placed himself. Admitting all these problems, Tillich nevertheless insists that it is possible and necessary to "distinguish between the *symbolic frame* in which the picture of Jesus as the Christ appears and the *substance* in which the power of the New Being is present" (*ST, 2,* 136–38; my italics). The frames are plural; the substance is singular. The substance is what makes the picture important, and what shines through the diverse frames as the substance is the power of the New Being. The substance is the important content of the picture, and the content is the power it mediates.

Tillich's highly ambiguous explanation of *analogia imaginis* can also be read in these terms. We have already seen that while he seems to suggest a formal analogy between the picture and the actual personal life that is its subject, in practice he supposes a formal analogy between the picture and the way in which power of being was mediated through that life. Close reading of the same passage, however, suggests that the real basis of the analogy lies not in the form of the picture, but in the power it conveys, for what *"implies* that there is an *analogia imaginis"* is the fact "that through this picture the New Being has *power* to transform those who are transformed by it." It was an actual personal life which "when encountered by the disciples . . . created the picture. And it was, and still is, this picture which mediates the transforming power of the New Being" (*ST, 2,* 114–15; my italics). What the picture and its subject have in common is not formal properties, but the power that each mediates.

Tillich's discussion of the material norm of theology can also be construed to mean that power is the most theologically important content of the biblical picture. We have seen that the material norm for theology is "the New Being in Jesus as the Christ as our ultimate concern." We have also seen that, as Tillich himself notes in one place, for theology today the material norm must be "the New Being in the Biblical picture of Jesus as the Christ as our ultimate concern."[1] Furthermore, Tillich thinks material norms have content, whose norm is "the Biblical message."[2] He refers to this content as the substance of the norms. Thus far it sounds as though the norm is some sort of "normative" idea or doctrine that would have intelligible content which can be stated more or less exactly in a straightforward way.

This is seriously misleading. Tillich makes it quite clear that "the message itself is beyond our grasp and never at our disposal (though it might grasp us and dispose of us)." Whatever it is, the content of the message cannot be stated in a straightforward way. Tillich goes on to suggest what sort of content this would be. Having claimed that his norm has the same substance as past norms, he says that this substance gives "an answer . . . to the question implied in our present situation." The question would be answered by a *"reality* of reconciliation and reunion." The symbol for this reality is New Being. The reality itself is manifested in Jesus the Christ.

It is important to note that what is manifested in Jesus the Christ is not the concept of New Being or a doctrine about reconciliation and reunion, but rather the reality of reconciliation and reunion. As we have seen, that reality is the reality of the presence of the power of New Being. Strictly speaking, such power is not an answer to an articulated question. It is, as Tillich himself often admits by his language, the ending of a quest. The important content of the picture is not some intelligible message that answers a request for information; it is a power that heals man and satisfies his deepest yearnings.

This is why the message is not within our grasp. A message whose

1. Cf. Tillich, "The Problem of Theological Method," p. 20.
2. For what follows, see *ST, 1,* 49–52.

content was specifiable information would be within our grasp and subject to our disposal, at least to the extent that we could assess whether it answered our question and decide whether we believed it. What clearly is not at our disposal is some life-transforming power. Such power is the content of the picture, and that is what makes the picture important to theology.

Finally, Tillich's account of how the biblical picture can bring all men to "participate" in Jesus as the Christ turns on the claim that the picture's content is power. He continues to use the analogy between the picture and a portrait in the expressionist style, but the very way he uses it undercuts its significance. He points out that, like an expressionist portrait, the picture speaks of Jesus' "experiences of loneliness and of meaninglessness and of his anxiety about the violent death which threatened him." However, "all of this is neither psychology nor the description of a character structure." The reports about Jesus do not psychologize; "more correctly, one could say that they ontologize." They "show only the presence of the power of New Being in him under the conditions of existence" (*ST*, *2*, 124). Thus, the biblical picture implies that the important content of Jesus is power. This power is not a function of his unique character or personality. On the contrary, while it may be present in Jesus in a uniquely complete way, still "in some degree all men participate in the healing power of New Being" (*ST*, *2*, 167).

Consequently, the biblical picture does not bring us to participation in Jesus as the Christ by bringing us to understand him most deeply as a person. Rather, it brings us to participate in "his own participation in God," which is to say that it brings us to share in a partial way the power of New Being in which he participated perfectly.

The picture does not have universal significance in the sense that it exhibits something true about all men, e.g. that God has established his covenant with them, or that they all share the same human predicament. Instead, the picture is universal because it can mediate the power of New Being to all men. It is not so much Jesus whom we "know" by the picture as the reality of this power in us. The analogy between the picture and Jesus is one not of form but of function. Both mediate the same power, and just as the important content of Jesus is the power of New Being, so too power is the theologically significant content of the biblical picture.

This claim is also made on analogy with what may be called "aesthetic entities." In this case, however, Tillich takes as his analogue a far broader spectrum of aesthetic works than mere painting. All "cultural creations," from the fine arts to a culture's language, have the same triad of elements: subject matter, form, and substance. "The form makes a cultural creation what it is. . . . In this sense it is the essence of a cultural creation." While form is deliberately intended, "substance can not be intended. It is unconsciously present in a culture, a group, an individual, giving passion and driving power to him who creates and the significance and power of meaning to his creations" (*ST, 3,* 60). Religious symbols like the biblical picture are "cultural creations"; their substance is the "driving power" of New Being.

The "Validity" of the Picture

According to Tillich, theology should criticize religious symbols as well as conceptualize and explain them. Where conceptualization of symbols consists in showing how various symbols and component symbols are interrelated, criticism involves showing how some symbols are more adequate than others. Criticism of the biblical picture consists in showing how and why it mediates power better than other symbols.

It is important to note at the outset that, in Tillich's view, religious symbols are not open to evaluation of their "truth." "Symbols . . . are not true or false in the sense of cognitive judgments."[3] Even if they correspond in some way with reality, this could not be checked "just because this reality is absolutely beyond human comprehension."[4] The difficulty does not arise from practical limitations on our observational techniques, like those that prevent us from confirming judgments about current events on Venus. Rather, the reality with which religious symbols would have to correspond is in principle inaccessible to any scrutiny precisely because it is not conditioned by any of the categories of experience and knowledge that we have.

Nonetheless, some sorts of evaluation of religious symbols are possible. Tillich summarizes these in the rest of a passage already quoted above:

> Symbols . . . are not true or false in the sense of cognitive judgments. But they are authentic or inauthentic with respect to their rise; they are adequate or inadequate with respect to their expressive power; they are divine or demonic with respect to their relation to the ultimate power of being.[5]

First, religious symbols may be "authentic or inauthentic with respect to their rise." Tillich's discussion makes it clear that to judge

3. Tillich, "Existential Analyses and Religious Symbols," p. 54.
4. Tillich, "The Religious Symbol," p. 28.
5. Tillich, "Existential Analyses and Religious Symbols," p. 104.

a symbol's authenticity is to judge whether it truly is a religious symbol. Note the reference to the rise of religious symbols. Tillich sometimes calls the truth of religious symbols "their adequacy to the religious experience they express." This does not mean that a symbol is authentic because it expresses a religious experience by giving an accurate description of it. Tillich shows this by going on to say, "Nonauthentic are religious symbols which have lost their experiential basis, but which are still used for reasons of tradition or because of their aesthetic value."[6] Religious symbols are adequate if used by people on the basis of their own religious experience. If not just the existence, but the use of the symbol rises out of this context, then the symbol is adequate; if not, then it is inadequate.

A religious symbol's adequacy is not just a function of its power to evoke the same experience in another person. Its adequacy is primarily a function of its being used in the right context, but it is a context in which the user has experienced the power of being and met the "holy." That is, the context is the context within which a symbol must be used if it is to be truly a religious symbol. When one evaluates the authenticity of a symbol, one is simply evaluating whether it is a religious symbol or some other kind.

Tillich sometimes says that the adequacy of religious symbols to religious experience is their "truth"; that is, the symbols are said to express a "knowledge" that is true. It is clear, however, that this knowledge is the knowledge given in revelation. It consists in certitude that one is in fact related to the power of being but does not give any positively correct information about what that power is like.[7] Thus, the "truth" conveyed by the symbol is the "truth" of

6. Tillich, "The Meaning and Justification of Religious Symbols," p. 10.
7. Tillich, "The Religious Symbol," p. 204.

indubitable expressions that make no fact-claims about the world, such as the expression, "I see green."

Secondly, religious symbols may be "adequate or inadequate with respect to their expressive power." The sort of adequacy meant here is presumably different from that discussed above. What is to be evaluated is not whether a symbol is used in a religious context, but whether it is effectively expressive. Tillich's test for adequacy in expressiveness seems to be entirely pragmatic: "Adequacy of expression means the power of expressing an ultimate concern in such a way that it creates reply, action, communication. Symbols which are able to do this are alive."[8] A symbol is adequate if it works, i.e. if it creates "reply, action, communication."

A symbol is "alive" (i.e. works) only "for a certain period, or in a certain place" when it "expressed truth of faith for a certain group."[9] Thus, the adequacy of a symbol's expressive power is measured solely by whether it serves to elicit "reply, action, communication" in a community. Whether it does depends on the group's reception of it and, apparently, not on any formal features of the symbol. The symbol seems to function in a causal way: it is a matter of empirical observation that the symbol does have a certain effect on a given group at a given time. To find out why, we apparently would have to analyze the group.

Thirdly, religious symbols may be "divine or demonic with respect to their relation to the ultimate power of being." Tillich's discussion of the distinction between "divine" and "demonic" regularly turns into a distinction between two ways in which a symbol can function. In Tillich's lexicon the "demonic" is the "destructive."

8. Tillich, *Dynamics of Faith,* p. 96.
9. Ibid., p. 16.

A religious symbol is demonic when it functions in a destructive way in the lives of those who receive it "idolatrously." In contrast, the "divine" is the presence of the unconditioned power of being. By definition, the presence of this power is ontologically healing. Hence, a religious symbol is divine when it mediates the power of being to the life of an estranged man.

Tillich seems to give two further criteria for distinguishing between demonic and divine symbols. The first is *formal*. A symbol is demonic when it fails to negate itself, when it tends to make itself final or offer itself as of ultimate value: "The claim of anything finite to be final in its own right is demonic" (*ST, 1,* 134). This is one way in which a demonic symbol is unlike a divine one with respect to their relation to the ultimate power of being. A divine symbol "points beyond itself" by virtue of certain of its formal features which indicate that the symbol itself is not to be taken as the focus of religious attention. A demonic symbol has formal features that make it self-referencing and direct religious attention to itself.

A demonic religious symbol is an "idol." Indeed, for Tillich, this is an analytical judgment. By definition, any religious symbol that is self-referencing is an idol: "It is the danger and an almost unavoidable pitfall of all religious symbols that they bring about a confusion between themselves and that to which they point. In religious language this is called idolatry."[10]

The second criterion by which to judge whether a symbol is divine or demonic is *pragmatic:* a symbol is demonic if it is destruc-

10. Tillich, "The Meaning and Justification of Religious Symbols," p. 10; cf. *Dynamics of Faith,* pp. 11–12, 97–98; *ST, 1,* 13.

tive of selves. When a man receives a demonic symbol in "faith," he tends to become ontologically disintegrated:

> The inescapable consequence of idolatrous faith is "existential disappointment," a disappointment which penetrates into the very existence of man! . . . the act of faith leads to a loss of the center and to a disruption of the personality.[11]

This is a second way in which a demonic symbol is unlike a divine one with respect to their relation to the ultimate power of being. A divine symbol effectively mediates the power of being to men, and this heals them. A demonic symbol is received as though it would mediate the power of being, but it does not and so is destructive of the person who received it.

Sometimes Tillich takes judgment of whether a symbol is divine or demonic to be the evaluation of the truth of religious symbols:

> in the realm of the religious symbols, the lack of truth is not error, but distortion, or to speak more exactly, it is demonic distortion or idolatry. The question of truth . . . is not the question of the existence or non-existence of a being.[12]

Here, "truth" is used in an odd way to mean "nondemonic" both in the sense of being not self-referencing and in the sense of being nondestructive.

In none of these three ways in which religious symbols may be evaluated is ontological analysis used as the source of criteria.

11. Tillich, *Dynamics of Faith,* p. 12. For an acute critical discussion of Tillich's notion of "idolatry," see William P. Alston, "Tillich on Idolatry," *Journal of Religion, 38* (1958), 4.
12. Tillich, "The Religious Symbol," pp. 205–06.

Tillich does not try to prove the truth of religious symbols independently of revelation by demonstrating the reality of their referent through ontological analysis, nor does he use ontology as the source of precise categories into which vague theological terms can be "translated." Ontology guarantees neither the truth nor the meaning of religious symbols. Judgments about whether a putative religious symbol is authentic, expressive, or divine are warranted by analysis of the revelatory events in which the symbols function.

The most that ontological analysis can do in the process of validating a religious symbol is provide backing for some of these warrants. It can show, for example, why one kind of finite entity is more suited than another to mediate the power of being. Historically, everything from trees and rocks to personalities and groups have functioned as religious symbols mediating the power of being. "Only in the last case do the symbols comprise the whole of reality," however. "For only in man are all dimensions of the encountered world united," from inorganic to spiritual. "It is therefore decisive for the rank and value of a symbol that its symbolic material be taken from the human person."[13] This ontological judgment backs some warrants about which symbols are most able to mediate the power of being, but it cannot show which symbols are in fact "true" in any sense of that term.

It is worth noting, in passing, that this particular backing puts dependent Christian revelations in an odd position. The miracle element in them is a verbal entity, a picture expressive of the occurrence of the original Christian revelation. Tillich has not offered an ontological analysis of narratives, but it is hard to see how, even

13. Tillich, "The Meaning and Justification of Religious Symbols," p. 11; cf. *ST, 1,* 118.

if they are reified to the point of being verbal icons, the narratives could be the ontological microcosms men are. On this basis the picture would have to be judged an inadequate occasioning symbol. This inadequacy would throw considerable doubt on the final and normative character of ongoing Christianity (i.e. dependent Christian revelations) in relation to other living religions. Surely this is an awkward conclusion for an apologetic argument!

The Issue

In the last two chapters we have discovered two quite different senses in which the biblical picture of Jesus as the Christ is said to have content, and one of them tends to be more important to Tillich than the other. As a verbal icon, as a symbol expressing the occurrence of the original Christian revelatory event, the picture's content is its formal structure. When Tillich discusses the nature of Christian theology, this is Scripture's theologically important content. Theology has the task of explicating the Christian message, which has answers for men's questions. Since Tillich feels that this content cannot be understood in terms of any kind of truth-claims or specific moral injunctions, he chooses to construe the message on the model of an aesthetic entity, a painting. Its determinate content, then, is its form, which can be described just as it is in itself. On the other hand, as the miracle element in dependent revelations, the picture's content is the power of New Being that it mediates. When Tillich undertakes to explain exactly what the Christian message is and how it answers men's questions, i.e. when he is actually doing theology, he makes power the theologically important content of the picture. This content cannot be described as it is in itself; it cannot be articulated. All that can be described is the effect the power has on man in his existential predicament. By subtly translating "questions" into "quests," "answers" into "healing," and "message" into "power," Tillich has made "power" rather than "form" the systematically decisive content of Scripture.

Given that the power mediated by the picture is more important to theology than the picture's form, how are form and power related? This is an important issue. The power mediated by the picture is important because without it the picture, while it might be of interest to historians of religion, would have no interest for theological reflection today. But if the content of the message communicated by the picture is simply identified with this power, the form of the picture would be theologically important only to the extent that it had some bearing on the picture's ability to mediate the power. If no such connection can be shown, then theology need not attend to the formal properties of the picture at all. Failure to show such a connection would create major problems for any theology constructed Tillich's way.

For one thing, it would effectively exclude Christology from systematic theology. As we have seen, Tillich denies that historical and apparent metaphysical fact-claims stated or implied in Scripture are authoritative for theology. Scripture is authoritative only when construed as a set of religious symbols, and especially when construed as yielding a picture of Jesus as the Christ. Since the fact-claims cannot be used, Tillich has to build his Christology on an analysis of the formal properties of the picture. If no connection can be shown between those formal properties and the power mediated by the picture, discussion of the picture's form becomes theologically irrelevant. The basis for doing Christology is removed, and theology is reduced to giving a phenomenological account of the effect of the power of New Being on men. Using a criterion entirely external to Tillich's system, one might wonder about the value of a method for doing Christian theology that, if followed consistently, makes Christology irrelevant.

So too, a failure to show a connection between the power and the form of the biblical picture would produce a serious incoherence within the structure of any theology done Tillich's way. Tillich has proposed a method by which Christian theology may be intelligibly done in the contemporary intellectual context. Its task is to explicate the distinctively Christian religious symbols because they are the expression of the occurrence of a final revelation. It was the form of the miracle element in the original revelation that made it final, for it was self-negating, and it is the form of the biblical picture that makes it the distinctively Christian symbol, for it is analogous to the form of the original miracle. Hence, theology is to explicate the determinate content, the formal structure, of the biblical picture of Jesus as the Christ precisely because it is Christian and is final.

This is of central theological importance. The symbolic expression of the original Christian revelation also functions as the miracle element in dependent Christian revelations. Precisely because it is the expression of the final revelation, it can serve there as the criterion by which to distinguish the merely religious or humanly subjective elements that men bring to dependent revelations and the genuinely revelatory element that breaks in on them as something new. If the formal features of the picture are theologically irrelevant, it will be impossible to distinguish respects in which the symbols express religious experiences and respects in which they express revelation. That means that it will be impossible to identify the data for theological argument!

Moreover, if the theologically important content of the picture is simply identified with the power it mediates, the form will be important only if its connection with the power is shown, for now it is asserted that the picture is to be explicated, not primarily because it is Christian or the expression of a past and final revelation, but because it is currently effective. Theology is solely concerned to reflect on what mediates the power of being in contemporary revelatory events. Unless the picture's form can be shown to have some connection with the picture's power, analysis of it becomes a non-theological enterprise. The task that was initially defined as the central task of Christian theology is now systematically excluded from theology. If no connection is shown between the form and the power of the picture, then we have a proposed method for constructing Christian theology that ends up making Christian theology an impossibility!

It is very important to be clear about what is *not* at issue here. We are not asking why one particular religious symbol was created instead of another, nor are we asking why this picture has the effect it has on some people and not on others. Traditionally, both questions have been answered by appeal to the Holy Spirit who "inspired" the Scriptures in the first place and continues to "illumine" some readers of Scripture so that it has a transforming effect on their lives. The Spirit is free, and no theologian would presume to explain why it does what it does. Seventeenth-century scholastic Protestant orthodoxy, however, went on to argue that a reason could be given for the ability that Scripture, properly understood under the Spirit's guidance, has to transform men's lives. This lies in the logical form of the scriptural accounts. They consist of historical and metaphysical fact-claims whose veracity is guaranteed by the Spirit's inspiration of the biblical writers. They are literally true. If the Spirit illumines a man's mind so that he can properly understand and thus accept them, these truths will have a liberating and regenerating effect on a man's life. Tillich quite rightly rejects this way of explaining the relation of the form of Scripture to its impact. We have no desire to make this outmoded tradition normative. We may agree that biblical scholarship makes this traditional treatment of the problem unacceptable today. Indeed, it may be a logical possibility that one could construct a theology in which the question of how the formal properties of Scripture are related to its impact on people does not even arise. However, given the method Tillich proposes for making theology accord with Scripture, the question does arise.

The Picture and the Spirit

It is clear that in principle neither Tillich's phenomenology of revelatory occurrences nor his ontological analysis nor biblical study can solve this problem. The phenomenology can describe only situations in which the picture does mediate power. The ontology can describe only the structure of human being that allows for existential disruption and the conditions under which it might be healed. Biblical study can describe only the formal structures that can be found in Scripture. Our thesis is that Tillich fails to provide a distinctively theological way by which the results of these different modes of investigation can be brought together and, as a result, his theological system is plagued with the difficulties discussed in the previous section. However, we need to examine Tillich's discussion of the Holy Spirit in which he attempts, as has more traditional theology, to show how meaning and power are related in the biblical picture of Jesus as the Christ. We contend that his discussion builds on an ambiguity in the term "meaning" and that this rises from Tillich's use of two incompatible "aesthetics."

Manifestations of the unconditioned power of being may be expressed by the term "Spirit" because they unite power and meaning (*ST, 1,* 111). The Spirit's presence is always mediated by ordinary words (*ST, 1,* 123; *3,* 127). When words are the vehicle of the Spirit, they increase in power. Ordinary language "does not possess the 'sound' and 'voice' which makes the ultimate perceivable," but under the impact of the Spirit language acquires this "sound" and "voice." "Language with this power is the 'Word of God' " (*ST, 1,* 124; *3,* 253–54).[14] When the Spirit uses language this way, it creates a symbol. Since the biblical picture is such a symbol, the combination of power and meaning that it has as God's Word must be a function of the union of power and meaning in the Spirit.

Tillich stresses that a necessary, though not sufficient, condition for language to have this power under the Spirit's impact is that it also be meaningful. For example, the "logical structure of ordinary language" is not destroyed; "nonsensical combinations of words do not indicate the presence of the divine." So too, he contends that in revelatory situations "something shines (more precisely, sounds) through ordinary language which is the self-manifestation of the *depth of being and meaning"* (*ST, 1,* 124; my italics). As we saw

14. For an important critique of Tillich's general theory of language from a Wittgensteinian point of view, see Paul L. Holmer, "Paul Tillich: Language and Meaning," *Journal of Religious Thought, 22* (1965–66), 85–107.

in the discussion of Tillich's ontology of the self, the depth of being and meaning is present in man's life as the depth of reason. It is an awareness of the set of absolutes (truth-itself, beauty-itself, justice-itself, etc.) which are the normative meanings of concepts used in all significant judgments. There is, then, a connection between the power the picture mediates and its meaning, such that the meaning it has is a necessary condition of its mediating the power.

The power of the picture taken as Word of God is identical with the power of the Spirit. This is true by definition. The picture, or any other set of words, becomes Word of God, i.e. has the requisite power, only when it is used under the impact of the Spirit. What the divine Spirit does to existentially estranged men it does only as mediated by words, and so the same result can equally well be ascribed to the words taken as Word of God.[15]

It is the power of the biblical picture of Jesus as the Christ that makes it important for theology for two reasons. First, the criterion of its being the Word of God is its effect on men: "it hits the human mind in such a way that an ultimate concern is created." Second, the picture is the norm for the kind of effect that is important: "Nothing is the Word of God if the effect it makes in a man contradicts the faith and love which are the work of the Spirit and which constitute the New Being as it is manifest in Jesus as the Christ" (*ST, 3,* 125) and pictured in the scriptural witness. This corroborates our earlier judgment that the most important content of the picture is its power.

But a necessary condition for the picture's having a powerful effect on men is its having meaning. What sort of meaning is this? Is the formal content of the picture identical with the meaning borne

15. E.g. cf. *ST, 3,* 252–65, and *1,* 147–55; *2,* 165–80.

by the Spirit, just as the power in the picture is identical with the power of the Spirit? The sense in which "meaning" is used here is always explained in terms of the effect the picture as Word of God has on men. For example, with respect to otherwise estranged interpersonal relations, "the Spirit-determined word . . . reaches the center of the other one by uniting the centers of the speaker and the listener" (*ST, 3,* 255). Enabling men to pierce the "shell of self-seclusion" in turn allows them to enter into relationships of authority over other men without reducing them to objects (*ST, 3,* 260–62). The Word of God has meaning for men in that it gives to otherwise fragmented and disordered lives coherence and a sense of significance. This may be called an axiological sense of meaning. The biblical picture as Word of God has meaning because it invests life with a felt-sense of its worthwhileness or valuableness.

Tillich speaks of meaning in precisely the same way in his discussion of the Logos. Logos is the religious symbol used to designate the "principle of divine self-manifestation in the ground of being itself" (*ST, 1,* 157). It is useful to construe Logos as a symbolic expression of just one aspect of the event expressed by "Spirit," viz., the meaning aspect, where "Abyss" is sometimes used to express the power aspect (*ST, 1,* 250, 156). Therefore, when one speaks of the Logos being manifested in Jesus as the Christ, one speaks especially of the meaning manifest there (*ST, 1,* 158). The meaning is to be understood not in terms of information but in terms of the effect on men's minds of the manifestation of Logos. It has the effect of giving a sense of unity to man's intellectual and cultural life, which otherwise seems to lack adequate norms, to be torn between absolutistic and relativistic frames of mind, and to be unable to integrate the formal and emotional sides of life (*ST, 1,* 147–55).

Logos, too, is said to bring meaning in an axiological sense of the term.

Tillich's doctrine of the Holy Spirit fails to show how form and power are related in the biblical picture. It does show that the power the picture has when functioning as the miracle element in dependent revelations is, in one sense of meaning, a meaning-bearing power. But it does not show at all how that function of the picture is related to its function as symbolic expression of the original Christian revelation, where its form is the picture's important content. His theology simply lacks any systematic way of relating these aspects of the picture.

Aesthetics as Warrant

Tillich construes the biblical witness to Jesus as a picture and says that it has a content whose meaning theology explicates. If the analogy between the biblical witness and a picture is to be very helpful, it will be necessary to specify more exactly the sense in which a picture, whether graphic or verbal, has meaning. An attempt to do this involves a theory of aesthetics. Judgments made in such a theory would then warrant judgments made about the content of the biblical picture of Jesus as the Christ. Tillich is not unaware of this. He often justifies judgments about the biblical picture by references to the way in which works of art have meaning.

The difficulty is that, on his own showing, the picture seems to have two quite different sorts of meaning. The meaning it has as the miracle element in dependent revelations can be specified only in terms of what it does to those who encounter it, and then it is described in axiological terms. The meaning the picture has as symbolic expression of an original revelation, however, is its formal structure which can be described just as it is. These two sorts of meaning are never related to each other. This problem seems to arise because Tillich runs together two quite incompatible aesthetics. One warrants judgments claiming the first kind of meaning in the picture, and the other warrants judgments claiming the second.

According to both aesthetics, the biblical picture of Jesus as the Christ is an expressive symbol. It does not consist of a description of anything. It is, to be sure, universal in significance, but its universality is a kind appropriate to a highly concrete verbal artifact. The two aesthetics differ completely in the way in which they understand the picture to be expressive.

Insofar as Tillich's theological judgments are warranted by analysis of the structure of the biblical picture, these warrants need the support of a "formalistic" aesthetic. Very generally, this would be the claim that criticism of works of art ought to attend primarily to their formal features, and not to what they seem to be "about," empirically speaking. Tillich sometimes adopts just such a position. He contends that "form should not be contrasted with content. The form which makes a thing what it is, is its content." Instead, it should be contrasted with the "material" of, say, a picture. The "material" is the collection of things or events that have their natural form and "are transformed by man's rational functions." Thus, "a landscape has a nature form which is, at the same time, its content. The artist uses the natural form of a landscape as material for an artistic creation whose content is not the material but rather what has been made of the material" (*ST, 1,* 178).[16] To explicate

16. For the background of Tillich's views on art in his early thought, see Adams, *Tillich's Philosophy of Culture, Science, and Religion,* Chap. 3.

that content, one analyzes the formal properties, the shape, that the artist has given his materials.

It is possible within the framework of a formalistic aesthetic to explain how a work of art is at once both concrete and universal. We have already seen how certain "new critics" do this in relation to works of literature. Rudolf Arnheim has shown how it is possible in the visual arts to combine the claim that form is content with the claim that every work of art is expressive. Relying on Gestalt psychology, which Tillich also relies on heavily, Arnheim contends that in works of the visual arts expression is embedded in structure. It is not that the form of movement of a line reminds us of an experience we have had previously. Rather, the form is immediately perceived by the observer in terms of strength, place, and distribution of various kinds of tension or forces.[17] What a painting or dance means is what it expresses, and that can be specified, not by describing its psychological effect on the observer ("It expresses sadness because it makes me sad"), but by describing the sort of forces perceived in its formal structure ("The shape, direction, and flexibility of its masses and lines convey an expression of passive hanging"). If an analogous argument could be developed for literary works, this aesthetic might illuminate how the biblical witness expresses a portrait of Jesus as the Christ. We can only note that Tillich does not show how such an aesthetic can be applied to works of literature.

When Tillich's theological judgments are warranted by description of the effect of the biblical picture on those who encounter it, a quite different aesthetic is used. The meaning of the picture is said

17. Rudolf Arnheim, "Expression," *Aesthetics Today,* ed. Morris Philipson (New York, Meridian Books, 1961), pp. 188–207.

to be its "spiritual substance." Here, form is contrasted with substance. A form is genuine, i.e. has such substance, if "it is an immediate expression of the basic experience out of which the artist lives" (*ST, 1,* 178–79).[18] The real meaning of the picture is something quite outside the picture, namely the "basic experience out of which the artist lives." The spiritual substance of the biblical picture of Jesus as the Christ is the power of New Being (*ST, 2,* 138), which is indeed the experience out of which the Gospel writers were living. Precisely because this is the meaning of the picture, it is necessary to negate the formal and material elements of the picture. This makes it possible for the picture to mediate something different from itself, viz., the power of being. On this view, biblical narratives can be compared to pictures only on the supposition that one looks "through" rather than "at" them in order to perceive beyond them the spiritual substance of which each is "the immediate expression" (*ST, 1,* 178–79). Tillich has adopted this position so much more often than he has taken the other that one cannot help concluding that it is his basic view on the question.[19]

This aesthetic assumes that a work of art must be both concrete and universal. The work of art achieves universality, not by any of its intrinsic features, but because it provides clues to a universe of memories and feelings that can be projected onto the object. In this view, as Arnheim puts it, "the visual pattern has as little to do

18. Cf. *ST, 3,* 60.
19. Cf. Paul Tillich, *The New Being* (New York, Charles Scribner's Sons, 1955), p. 133; *The Religious Situation* (New York, Henry Holt & Co., 1932), pp. 41, 53–54; "Art and Ultimate Reality," *Art and the Craftsman,* eds. Joseph Harned and Neil Goodwin (New Haven, *Yale Literary Magazine,* 1961), pp. 185–200.

with the expression we confer upon it as words have to do with the content they transmit."[20]

This is an extremely problematical aesthetic. It has been under serious attack at least since the day James McNeill Whistler scandalized art criticism of his time by complaining that "people have acquired the habit of looking . . . not *at* a picture, but *through* it, at some human fact, that shall, or shall not, from a social point of view, better their mental or moral state"[21] (or, we might add, their ontological state). The "new critics" have attacked the same view when applied to literature. Allen Tate has pointed out that Poe, for example, in his more metaphysically inclined prose, tries to express imaginatively that which is beyond the world of nature by directing our attention away from finite natural things. Tate calls this the "angelic" use of the imagination because it tries to apprehend metaphysical truth directly, without going through sense experience. Poe's attempt fails:

> Since he refuses to see nature, he is doomed to see nothing. He has overleaped and cheated the condition of man. The reach of our imaginative enlargement is perhaps no longer than the ladder of analogy, at the top of which we may see all, if we still wish to *see* anything, that we have brought up with us from the bottom, where lies the sensible world. If we take nothing *with us* to the top but our emptied, angelic intellects, we shall see nothing when we get there.[22]

20. Arnheim, "Expression," p. 191.
21. James A. McNeill Whistler, *Ten O'Clock, A Lecture* (Portland, Me., Thomas Bird Mosner, 1916), pp. 5–6.
22. Tate, *Man of Letters*, p. 131.

Regardless of the validity of this as criticism of Poe, it is suggestive in connection with Tillich. On Tillich's grounds, the biblical picture is a work of the angelic imagination. One ought to "crucify" everything that is in the picture in order to apprehend what is beyond it— and beyond all experience. The question immediately arises whether, since we bring nothing from the picture with us, we shall in fact see anything when we look beyond it.

Conclusion

Tillich has proposed to make Scripture authoritative for theology by construing it as an aesthetic entity. It is important for theology only insofar as it contains a picture of Jesus as the Christ. Theology is to explicate the content of this picture.

This proposal quite literally falls apart in practical application. The meaning of the picture is supposed to be the data authorizing theological judgments, but running through Tillich's theology is an equivocation in the way "meaning" is used. In practice there seem to be two authoritative pictures. On one hand, there is the picture that is meaningful in the sense that it has a powerful impact on men's lives, making them meaningful. Theological judgments based on this picture as data are warranted by analysis of revelatory events, but an analysis that attends solely to the picture's function in dependent revelations, viz., its function as miracle. These warrants are supported by an aesthetic that finds the meaning of works of art in experiences extrinsic to the works themselves. On the other hand, there is the picture that is meaningful in the sense that it has a determinate, intelligible structure that can be described just as it is in itself and without reference to its effect on the beholder. Theological judgments based on this picture are also warranted by analysis of revelations, but by that part of the analysis that attends to the picture's function in original revelations, viz., its function as symbolic expression of the occurrence of that event. Use of these warrants is based on a quite different aesthetic that finds the meaning of works of art intrinsic to the works themselves.

As a result, theological reflection on the biblical picture of Jesus as the Christ seems to come up with two different sets of judgments that are not logically related to each other at all. No systematic connection between them has been shown either by ontological analysis or by any theological move, such as the claim that the divine Spirit also unites meaning and power. Furthermore, Tillich gives systematic priority to the picture as mediator of power. Its formal features are theologically important only if it can be shown that they somehow explain its ability to mediate power, and no such thing is ever shown.

7

"GOD" AS RELIGIOUS SYMBOL: A TEST CASE

Tillich's discussion of "God" is an occasion both to review and to test our proposals about the fabric of Tillich's theology. We have suggested how phenomenological description of revelatory events, ontological analysis, historical research, and aesthetics are interwoven in Tillich's conceptualizing, explaining, and criticizing of the data for Christian theology. Does this scheme also describe how he explicates the meaning of "God"?[1] We have proposed that when he uses scriptural material as data for theological argument he construes it on an aesthetic model. Will this fit the way he explicates the meaning of the term "God," which is certainly less obviously iconic than the picture of Jesus as the Christ?

Before we can pursue these questions fruitfully, we must note a possible source of confusion in Tillich's complex use of "God." He consistently assumes that his task as a Christian theologian is to explicate the view that God is triune. He distinguishes between the Christian doctrine of the Trinity and the "trinitarian principles" which are its presuppositions (*ST, 1,* 250). We shall argue that

1. Hereafter we shall use "God" to designate the word and the word God to designate the reality.

explanation and criticism of the Christian use of "God" occur when Tillich deals with the trinitarian principles and that conceptualization occurs when he deals with the distinctively Christian doctrine of the Trinity. In these discussions, "God" is used in at least two ways. Often it is used for what traditionally has been called the Godhead. When he discusses "God as Living," Tillich talks about the trinitarian principles present in the idea of God, which suggests that "God" is not the name of just one of the Persons of the Triune Godhead (*ST, 3,* 285). However, in the first volume of his *Systematic Theology* when he discusses "God as Creating," he seems to be explicating only the doctrine of the First Person of the Trinity. He expressly says that the symbol of "God as creator" contains the answer to man's question about his finitude, and he puts this in parallel with "Jesus as the Christ" as the answer to man's question about his estrangement and with the "Spirit" as the answer to man's question about the ambiguity of his life (*ST, 3,* 286; *1,* 204–08). In short, what a great many commentators on Tillich fail to observe is that a large part of what is usually referred to as Tillich's doctrine of God is really only his treatment of the First Person of the Trinity. This means that, insofar as Tillich's concern is to explicate the distinctively Christian symbol for God, his doctrine of God in Part II of his theology is only part of his discussion of "God."

Explanation of "God"

The theologian's task of explanation is to show "the relation of the symbols used to that to which they point." In respect to God, Tillich seems to go about it in two quite different ways.

When he is discussing the "actuality of God," Tillich equates "God" with the unconditioned.

Many confusions in the doctrine of God and many apologetic weaknesses could be avoided if God were understood first of all as being-itself or as the ground of being. (*ST, 1,* 235)

nothing can be said about God theologically before the statement is made that he is the power of being in all beings. (*ST, 3,* 294)

Such statements lead critics to charge, in a somewhat general way, that his "ontology is . . . the controlling concept in Tillich's system, and one which dictates the form of every theological statement made."[2] Kenneth Hamilton states the criticism more precisely when he claims that in Tillich's hands explicating the meaning of words found in the Christian message consists in "a process of taking words from there (e.g. 'God' and 'grace') and of translating them into the technical terms" provided by ontology.[3] The complaint is that ontology "controls" theological statements by purporting to give the precise meaning of traditional terms that hitherto have been used vaguely. This means that before the simple believer could claim to have heard the Christian message properly he would have to understand Tillich's ontology! There is no point in denying that Tillich provides a great deal of evidence to support this interpretation of his method.

The issue turns on whether "God" is to be understood as a proper name. Tillich tells us that "the statement that God is being-itself is

2. McKelway, *Systematic Theology of Tillich,* pp. 237–38; cf. W. R. Rowe, "The Meaning of 'God' in Tillich's Theology," *Journal of Religion, 42* (1962), 280 ff.
3. Hamilton, *The System and the Gospel,* p. 26.

a non-symbolic statement" (*ST, 1,* 238). "God" is a proper name, and the ontological analysis in which being-itself is given meaning also gives the meaning of "God." We need not settle the question whether proper names refer but have no "sense," i.e. cannot be given definitions, or both refer and have sense, or both refer and presuppose, but without asserting, the "truth of certain uniquely referring descriptive statements."[4] Perhaps ontological analysis explains the meaning of "God" by offering a definition in terms of being-itself. More likely, since the nature of the unconditioned power of being is in principle unknowable even by ontology, ontological analysis explains the meaning of "God" by specifying its referent as being-itself, the unconditioned power of being whose presence ontology can point out without describing. Once "God" is explained in this straightforward way, it is possible for theology to state additional information about God or being-itself. All terms used as predicates in such statements will be used symbolically, for everything said about God beyond the fact that he is being-itself is symbolical (*ST, 1,* 239).[5] However, Tillich seems to hold that since we can state in direct fashion who or what God is ("God is being-itself"), we can claim to have some idea how the terms used symbolically

4. John R. Searle, "Proper Names," *Philosophy and Ordinary Language,* ed. Charles E. Caton (Urbana, University of Illinois Press, 1963), pp. 154–62.

5. It must be added that in the second volume of the *ST* Tillich changes his position. There he says that the only nonsymbolic assertion about God is "the statement that everything we say about God is symbolic" (*ST, 2,* 9). But this clearly is not a statement about God, but about *statements,* namely, statements about God. It is a piece of second-order discourse. If this is the position Tillich wants to take, it further supports our position that in his theology traditional religious terms like "God" are *not* explained by being translated into ontological terminology, for, if this is Tillich's final position, it appears that no "translation" of "God," no ontological identification of who or what "God" refers to, is possible.

("God has 'power' over the world") apply. In this way, "God" is explained by using ontology to show how the symbol is related to that to which it points.

There is a second, quite different way in which Tillich explains the term "God." It shows the proper context in which to use the term, rather than identifying or describing its referent. It relies on warrants yielded by analysis of revelations rather than warrants produced by ontology. "God" turns out not to be a name in any ordinary sense of the term at all. It is used to express the occurrence of a revelatory event. It is not used to specify any quality of the event or of any of the component elements in the event, so it cannot be used to describe or classify anything. Nor is it used like a proper name. One of the essential elements of the revelatory event it expresses is the ecstasy of the receiver of the revelation. That can only be confessed and cannot be identified independently by someone else. Hence, unlike the referent of a proper name, the unique referent of "God" cannot be ostensively shown.

These claims about a second way in which Tillich treats "God" are based on a number of passages that are usually ignored or underemphasized in discussions of his doctrine of God. We shall note them here in some detail.

Tillich divides his discussion of God in Part II of his *Systematic Theology* into an account of "The Meaning of 'God' " and an account of "The Actuality of God." His account of the meaning of "God" explains the term by showing how it is related to the revelatory events that it expresses or "points to." "God . . . is the term for that which concerns man ultimately." What concerns man ultimately must be concrete, for "it is impossible to be concerned about something which cannot be encountered concretely" (*ST, 1,* 211). In its concreteness, it must be experienced as holy. What concerns man ultimately must also "transcend every preliminary finite and concrete concern"; this is the "divine" (*ST, 1,* 211–15), the unconditioned power that determines our "being or not-being" (*ST, 1,* 14). A situation in which both the concrete and the transcendent, both the holy and the divine, are found is by definition a revelatory event. "God" is not used to name either the power of being that is present or the holy object alone, or even the event as a historical reality. Rather, it is used to express the fact that a revelatory event has taken place *for* someone who himself was one of the elements correlated in the event.

At the heart of Tillich's account of the reality of God is a discussion of "God as Living." Here he makes it explicitly clear that "God" is explained by showing that it is used to express the occurrence of revelatory events. He begins by distinguishing between the use of ontological categories as concepts and their use as symbols. "Life" is an ontological category which, carefully defined and used conceptually, can be employed to describe one of the most general features of human experience. When analyzed, it yields the self–world distinction and the polar elements which can also be used conceptually to describe general features of experience. When predicated of God, however, the same terms are used as symbols and not as definable categories (*ST, 1,* 242).[6] In this way, "the ontological structure of being supplies the material for the symbols which point to the divine life." However, Tillich stresses, *"this does not mean that a doctrine of God can be derived from an ontological system. The character of the divine life is made manifest in revelation"* (*ST, 1,* 243; my italics). If theology wishes to explain the term

6. It is repeated in *ST, 3,* 417.

"God," it must relate it not to ontological categories, but to the revelatory event that it expresses.

Tillich then shows that the trinitarian principles found in almost every known use of "God" are direct functions of the dynamics of revelatory events. "Human intuition of the divine has always distinguished between the abyss of the divine (the element of power) and the fullness of its content (the element of meaning), between the divine depth and the divine *logos.*" The depth is the power of being; the Logos is "the principle of God's self-objectification" that makes the fullness of the power of being "distinguishable, definite, finite." Once again we have the claim that "God" expresses both the presence of transcendent power and a concrete mediator of that power. But from analysis of revelations we know that man's "intuition of the divine" occurs only in particular happenings. Hence the third principle always distinguished in man's intuition of the divine is the actualization of the other two in a way that makes them "creative." Tillich uses the ontological term "spirit" as a symbol to express this third principle. As an ontological concept it designates dimensions of reality in which power and meaning are united; used as a symbol (distinguished by an uppercase "S"), it expresses a creative occurrence in which power and meaning are united.

Indeed, while "Spirit" may be used to express one of the three principles, it is also used as "the most embracing, direct, and unrestricted symbol" (*ST, 1,* 249) for the divine life. If, in the first way of explaining the term, "God is being-itself" is the most comprehensive nonsymbolic utterance that can be made about "God," then, in the second way the term is explained, "God *is* Spirit" is the most comprehensive symbolic utterance that can be made. It would seem, in fact, that "God" and "Spirit" are entirely inter-

changeable, for the best way to explain "God" is to explain "Spirit."
It shows that "God" is not used to name either depth or Logos alone,
but to express their combination in a particular creative occurrence.

Tillich makes the same point in other passages both outside and
within the system. In one essay he says, "The term 'ultimate reality'
is not another name for God in the religious sense of the word." To
be sure, "the God of religion would not be God if he were not first
of all ultimate reality." Nevertheless, "the God of religion is more
than ultimate reality."[7] In his very important article, "The Two
Types of Philosophy of Religion," he makes the same point and
explains what "more" there is in "God" than "ultimate reality":
"God is unconditioned, that makes him God; but the 'unconditional'
is not God. The word 'God' is filled with the concrete symbols in
which mankind has grasped its ultimate concern," i.e. has expressed
"its being grasped by something unconditional."[8] "God" is used
to express revelatory events in which the unconditioned power of
being is present not in a "pure" state, but only as mediated by concrete symbols. "God" is an expression, not of the power of being
alone, but of the occurrence of events in which power is made present through concrete symbols.

Tillich makes this point within the system when, in the second
volume of his *Systematic Theology,* he attempts to restate the difference between his view of God and traditional "supernaturalism"
and religious "naturalism." These views treat "God" as a name
interchangeable with the name of the ontologically ultimate principle. Supernaturalism identifies God with a particular being, "the

7. Tillich, "Art and Ultimate Reality," p. 186.

8. Paul Tillich, "The Two Types of Philosophy of Religion," *Theology of
Culture,* pp. 24–25.

highest being," separated "from all other beings, alongside and above which he has his existence."[9] Religious naturalism identifies God with "the creative ground of all natural objects," and hence "the term 'God' becomes interchangeable with the term 'universe' and therefore is semantically superfluous."

The reasons Tillich gives for rejecting supernaturalism and naturalism are drawn, not from an ontological analysis showing their invalidity as metaphysics, but from analysis of the dynamics of revelations. Supernaturalism is inadequate because, by equating God with a particular being, it identifies God with something conditioned and therefore finite. This violates the rule that "God" be used in relation to that which transcends the finite realm and which can be the object of genuinely ultimate concern. Religious naturalism is rejected because it identifies "God" with an abstraction. This violates the rule that God be used in relation to that which, while transcendent, is also concrete enough to be the object of concern and to be experienced as holy.

As an alternative, Tillich offers a "self-transcendent" or "ecstatic" view of God. By this he seems to mean that "God" expresses in one way a fact that ontological analysis describes in another, viz., the fact that the world is "self-transcending." Ontological analysis shows that the world is at once "substantially independent of the divine ground" and "that it remains in substantial unity with it." In their dialectical relationship, the world and its ground constitute "one reality which . . . is experienced in different dimensions which point to one another."

It can be experienced in terms of the quests men have. Tillich repeatedly makes the point that the dialectical relation between

9. For what follows, see *ST, 2,* 6–9.

world and ground is the necessary condition for these quests. Men could not ask questions if they were not at once separated from the truth, so that they have to ask, and united with it, so that they know enough to ask. Men could not quest for ontological healing if they were not estranged from the power of being, and yet they must be united with it or they would not have enough reality to quest. In these and other ways men transcend themselves, questing for what they lack. Tillich holds that this ontological description of man as questing is stated in nonsymbolic terms. It does not speak of God directly or describe the divine ground, for it is an "x"-we-know-not-what. It speaks only in terms of man's quest and refers to God only in terms of the effects that are sought, viz., the presence of that power that can end man's quests.

The dialectical relationship between world and divine ground can also be experienced in terms of the presence of that power which ends man's quests. "In terms of immediate experience it is the encounter with the holy, an encounter which has an ecstatic character." This is a revelatory event. "God" is used not to name the unconditioned power of being, but to express the occurrence of an event in which this power is encountered in a holy object by a man in ecstasy. What ontological analysis could describe only in terms of a need and a yearning, religious symbolism expresses in terms of the experience on a particular occasion of a felt transformation of the self.

In none of these passages has Tillich explained the term "God" by treating it like a proper name and using ontology to identify or describe its unique referent. It is not used to name the power of being; ontology can do that (being-itself, power of being). It is not used to name some holy object through which that power is mediated; there are other terms for that ("Jesus," "Totem," "Zeus").

It is not used to name the revelatory event in which healing power and holy object are combined; historical terms do that ("Exodus from Egypt," "Crucifixion of Jesus"). Rather, "God" is used to express (that is Tillich's term with all its aesthetic overtones) the fact that a revelatory event has occurred *for someone*. In order to show how "God" is related to that to which it points, Tillich has described the *use* of the term, and the warrants for judgments about the proper use of the term derive from analysis of the dynamics of revelatory events.

The inconsistency in Tillich's explanation of the content of the biblical picture of Jesus as the Christ is repeated in an almost identical way in his explanation of "God." Just as the content of the picture sometimes was said to be the power that it mediates, so too, the meaning of "God" is sometimes identified with its referent, the power of being. This happens when Tillich uses ontological warrants to support his explanation, and it has led to the charge that he has the fallacious view that the meaning of a word is the thing it designates.[10] Sometimes the content of the picture was said to be its expression of the miracle element in the original Christian revelation. So too,

10. Cf. John Y. Fenton, "Being-Itself and Religious Symbolism," *Journal of Religion, 45* (1965), 73–86. In two of his studies of Tillich's theory of language Paul L. Holmer supposes that Tillich unambiguously takes "God" to be a concept rather than a religious symbol; see "Paul Tillich and the Language About God," *Journal of Religious Thought, 22* (1965–66), 35–51, and "Paul Tillich: Language and Meaning." Robert P. Scharlemann, in "Tillich's Method of Correlation: Two Proposed Revisions," *Journal of Religion, 46,* Pt. 2 (January 1966), 92–104, and Ford, in "The Three Strands of Tillich's Theory of Religious Symbols," both recognize that Tillich uses "God" in the two quite different ways we have noted; Scharlemann in particular makes observations about the difficulties this creates for a theology designed exclusively to explain, criticize, and conceptualize religious symbols.

"God" is sometimes explained in terms of its expressive function. We shall examine a bit later whether "expression," when it is used of "God," has the aesthetic connotations it had in connection with the biblical picture; if so, the analogy between the inconsistency in explaining the picture and in explaining "God" is nearly perfect. In any case, just as the two ways in which the picture was explained were never related, so too, the two ways in which "God" is explained are never expressly related. Since they suppose quite different logics for the use of "God," they are probably mutually exclusive. The most that can be said is that if we ignore the first way of explaining "God" and rely entirely on the second it is possible to offer an internally consistent interpretation of Tillich's theory that generally "saves the data" and is in accord with his dictum that theology's task is to interpret religious symbols. If, with most of his commentators, one insists that the first way of explaining "God" is Tillich's central theological method, then his theology turns out to be an explication of ontological mysteries, and large sections of his *Systematic Theology,* where symbols are explicated, must be discarded as irrelevant to the theological task.

Criticism of "God"

In criticizing a religious symbol, a theologian seeks to show how some symbols are more adequate and how others are inadequate to the encounter they express. Tillich's criticism of "God" is designed to show that only a trinitarian use of "God" is adequate. The warrants for the critical judgments are drawn from analysis of revelatory events, for "the substance of all trinitarian thought is given in revelatory experiences" (*ST, 3,* 286).

We have seen that, speaking descriptively, Tillich holds that "God" is used to express that which is at once concrete and ultimate. He uses this, however, as the basis for a prescriptive judgment about how "God" ought to be used. He distinguishes between "mystical" and "polytheistic" ways of using "God" which are inadequate and the trinitarian way of using "God" which is adequate.

Mystical monotheism "transcends all realms of being and value, and their representatives, in favor of the divine ground and abyss from which they come and in which they disappear," with the result that "the element of ultimacy swallows the element of concreteness." This is an inadequate way to use "God." In actual practice it is "not able to suppress the quest for concreteness" and so is wide open for the reintroduction of polytheism, which emphasizes the element of concreteness at the expense of the element of ultimacy. "God" ought not to be used exclusively in the way names for abstractions ("ground of being") are used, for then religion becomes unstable.

In polytheistic religions, "God" is used to refer to concrete beings that "lack . . . a uniting and transcending element." This is an unstable use of "God" because it "leads to conflicting claims and threatens to destroy the unity of the self" that has taken such concrete things as the determiners of its "being or not-being." "God" should not be used in the way proper names are used.

The only adequate use of "God" is one that exhibits trinitarian elements, for the trinitarian use of "God" is "an attempt to speak of . . . the God in whom the ultimate and the concrete are united" (*ST, 1*, 222–28). The distinctively Christian doctrine of the Trinity is only one of several uses of "God" that exhibits these trinitarian elements. It arises out of the distinctively Christian revelatory event, the manifestation of the power of being in Jesus as the Christ. Since

Tillich takes this to be the final or normative revelatory event, the Christian use of "God" is the most adequate of all the trinitarian ways of using "God."

Conceptualization of "God"

The distinctively Christian use of "God," i.e. the "developed trinitarian doctrine in Christian theology," is the product of "the manifestation of the divine ground of being in the appearance of Jesus as the Christ" (*ST, 3,* 285).[11] The three persons of the Trinity correlate with the three ways in which that revelation answers man's questions.

> The questions arising out of man's finitude are answered by the doctrine of God and the symbols used in it. The questions arising out of man's estrangement are answered by the doctrine of Christ and the symbols applied to it. The questions arising out of the ambiguities of life are answered by the doctrine of the Spirit and its symbols. (*ST, 3,* 286)

We have noted several times that what Tillich calls answers to man's questions is best understood as power that ends man's quests for ontological healing. This power is mediated in Christian revelations and is expressed in religious symbols. Theological doctrines are discussions of these symbols. Consequently, it seems fair to gloss the above as follows. Each of the persons of the Trinity is a religious symbol expressive of one aspect of the complex event of ontological healing that takes place in a Christian revelatory event, and the

11. Cf. *ST, 1,* 250.

doctrines of God qua creator (Vol. 1), Christ (Vol. 2), and Spirit (Vol. 3), respectively, discuss each of these symbols. To this we may add another point already noted, viz., that "Spirit," or, as Tillich far more frequently uses it, "Spiritual Presence," is the most embracing symbol for God, the symbol that expresses all three of these aspects together. This must be understood, furthermore, in the context of our observation that "God (qua creator)" and "Christ" express aspects abstracted from the concrete event that is expressed in its wholeness by "Spirit."

We may then conclude that the task of conceptualizing the term "God" consists in showing the pattern of relations that obtain among the three main component symbols, "God (qua creator)," "Christ," and "Spirit," and *their* respective component symbols. For example, Tillich holds that "Christ" is subordinate to "Spirit." "Spirit" expresses the presence of the power of being wherever it is found (*ST, 3,* 147). It is only because this power was also found in Jesus that it can be said, "God was in Him" (*ST, 3,* 144). "Christ" is the symbol used to express one aspect of the original Christian revelation, viz., the fact that this ontological healing power was mediated by Jesus. To be sure, since this power was present in Jesus "without distortion," original Christian revelation was the normative or final manifestation of the power of being. This one revelatory event provides the criteria by which to measure how far the power is truly present elsewhere. Hence, for the purposes of our religious talk, proper use of "Christ" is the criterion to which use of "Spirit" is subordinated (*ST, 3,* 148).[12] Nevertheless, "Christ" expresses only one aspect of the event which is expressed in its totality by "Spirit."

12. Cf. ibid., *3,* 125.

Tillich is less clear about how "God (qua creator)" is related to "Spirit." Much of his discussion of the actuality of God is warranted by ontology and not by analysis of the Christian revelatory event, so it does not stand in parallel with his explication of "Christ" and the "Spirit." However, there is evidence that in effect he subordinates "God (qua creator)" to "Spirit" or "Spiritual Presence." "God as originating creator" is the religious symbol the Christian message uses to express the revealed answer to the question of finitude, which is not to be confused with the question of estrangement. It does not have to do with how to overcome the ontological disruption that comes with estrangement. It has to do with how one continues to get the power of being which one would need continually to receive even if one were not estranged. The doctrine of God is the answer to this question in the sense that "God (qua creator)" expresses the event in which this power is received (*ST, 1,* 253–54). Talk about "God's sustaining creativity" expresses one aspect of the reception of this power, viz., the continuing "over-againstness" of the receiver of the power to the power (*ST, 1,* 261). Terms like "God's directing creativity" or "providence" express another aspect of the same event, viz., the felt-experience of a "quality which 'drives' or 'lures' " every constellation of conditions "toward fulfillment," such that one courageously acts in the faith that "no situation whatsoever can frustrate the fulfillment of his ultimate destiny" (*ST, 1,* 267).

All this must be understood in the context of the claim that in actual fact this power is not received except in occurrences which are also ontologically healing. Thus, an event that is expressed by "Christ" in respect of its being a healing or saving event is expressed by "God (qua creator)" in respect of its also being a sustaining event. This in turn must be understood in the context of Tillich's further claim that "Spirit" is used to express the total event, since the event makes *actual* in somebody's life a union of power (creative, sustaining) and meaning (restored significance and coherence to what was broken).

In an important essay, Tillich himself provides just this gloss for his discussion of "God." In "Existential Analysis and Religious Symbols," he suggests that man's sense of his failure to affirm himself ontically is expressed by the mythological symbol of "man as a creature." At the same time, the symbol of creation expresses finite man's "participation in [his] own infinite ground"; or, "more existentially expressed, the symbol of creation shows the source of the courage to affirm one's own being in terms of power and meaning in spite of the very present threat of non-being." He goes on to show how other symbols like "omnipotence, omnipresence, and providence" express the same occurrence.

The same essay provides a parallel gloss on Tillich's discussion of "Christ." He proposes that "sin" expresses man's sense of failing to affirm his own essential nature. When this anxiety is "amalgamated with the anxiety of finitude," it is expressed in symbols such as "judgment, condemnation, punishment, and hell." Man's participation in an event that heals this ontological disruption is "mythologically expressed in symbols such as salvation, redemption, regeneration, and justification, or in personal symbols such as saviour, mediator, Messiah, Christ."

Tillich's point in this article is that each of these symbols is used to express one aspect or another of a complex occurrence for which the all-embracing symbol is "God."[13] Here, "God" is used not in the restricted sense as the First Person of the Trinity, but for the

13. Tillich, "Existential Analyses and Religious Symbols," pp. 48–54.

Godhead, for which Tillich elsewhere says "Spirit" is the most all-embracing symbol. In terms used earlier, this suggests that these several symbols are component symbols, together constituting the symbol "God." Conceptualization of "God" thus consists in tracing out the patterns of relations among these component symbols.

This sugests that, like the biblical picture of Jesus as the Christ, "God" may be understood on the model of an aesthetic entity, a product of the religious imagination characterized by a describable form or structure. Tillich never expressly puts it this way, but the points already noted seem to allow for such a reading when combined with some additional pieces of evidence.

When Tillich is laying out his general theory of religious symbols, he distinguishes between primary and secondary symbols. Secondary symbols are material things like water, light and oil, or poetic and metaphoric expressions that do not have peculiarly religious uses in and of themselves, but sometimes are used as parts of religious symbols. Primary symbols, however, quite clearly are imaginative and verbal. They establish a "highest" being and attribute characteristics to him; they speak of divine actions; and they consist in accounts of divine manifestations and incarnations.[14] Furthermore, when Tillich is explaining how "God" is properly used to express that which is at once concrete and transcendent, he expressly notes that the concrete reality need not be something in the "realm of reality" but may equally well be in the "realm of imagination" (*ST, 1,* 211).

"God" may be used to express an imaginatively rendered entity that is specified by the recital of stories in which "God" is the chief agent. The stories might be as brief as " 'God' created the world"

14. Tillich, "The Meaning and Justification of Religious Symbols," pp. 8–9.

or " 'God' saves mankind." Tillich calls such narrative religious symbols "myths." If our exposition and analysis of his position have been correct, it would seem fair to say that they are rather precise ways of expressing the occurrence of a revelatory event by expressing the occurrence of the event as a whole: "God"; and then expressing some one aspect of it precisely as a part of the more complex whole: "creation" or "salvation." On these grounds, Yahweh, the chief figure in the stories imaginatively recited by ancient Israel about its involvement in a history of saving and revealing events, functions in the same way as "God." One can best point out the meaning of Israel's stories, e.g. "Yahweh brought us out of Egypt with a mighty hand," by showing what facets of Israel's saving events are expressed by the component symbols making up the story. On the same grounds, it is perfectly proper for a Christian who receives Jesus in ecstasy to say of him, "My Lord and my God!" It is precisely in the presence of Jesus as the Christ that the entire occurrence of salvation–revelation takes place for the Christian. When he uses "God" in relation to Jesus as the Christ, he is not describing some unique ontological property of Jesus. Rather, he is expressing his experience of the holy in Jesus and his reception of the transcendent power of being through Jesus. Moreover, it would be proper for him to tell a story by stringing some symbols together: " 'God' was in Christ reconciling the world to himself." This would simply be a more precise expression of certain aspects of a saving event. It would express the occurrence of the event as a whole: "God!" It would specify what had served as the miracle element in the event: "Jesus as the Christ!" It would express in particular the healing of one aspect of ontological disruption: "reconciliation!"

It is also possible to combine religious symbols with "God" in sentences that look like descriptions of a being called "God," e.g. "God is transcendent." This once again brings to a head the issue of whether the warrants for explication of such utterances come from ontological analysis or from analysis of revelatory events. If the sentence is construed as some sort of description, then one must appeal to ontology both to justify and to explain the description in clear and precise language. But it need not be construed that way. It may be understood as a symbolic expression of a revelatory event. Its meaning may be explicated by showing how its component symbols are interrelated, and the warrants for these judgments would derive from analysis of revelations. Tillich says that "God is transcendent" means that "within itself, the finite world points beyond itself, in other words, is self-transcendent" (*ST, 2,* 7). However, it means this only when it functions to express the revelatory event in which this self-transcending of the finite world is a matter of immediate and saving experience. "The world is self-transcendent" is, for Tillich, a straightforward, nonsymbolic assertion purporting to describe an ontological state of affairs, but it cannot simply be substituted for "God is transcendent" every time the latter is used. Precisely because it uses "God," the sentence "God is transcendent" is not a straightforward, nonsymbolic assertion. It does not describe either a state of affairs in the world or an entity called "God." Rather, it is a symbolic expression of the occurrence of a saving event. It expresses the event as a whole: "God"; then it expresess one aspect of the whole, in this case the self-transcending of the miracle element in the event, i.e. the fact that it mediated the unconditioned power of being: "transcendent!"

Analysis of Tillich's discussion of "God" not only reviews in short compass our proposals about the fabric of Tillich's theology but also tends to confirm them. His discussion of the actuality of God provides the one significant place in his *Systematic Theology* where he directly translates religious talk using "God" into technical ontological discourse. In these passages, his judgments about God are warranted by ontological analysis. However, even in this section, and consistently in the rest of the *Systematic Theology*, there are passages where the warrants for his judgments are provided by analysis of revelatory events. Moreover, even though Tillich has never described the Christian use of "God" as an act of "picturing," these passages suggest that "God" be explicated as an aesthetic work of the imagination. One result of the use of these two diverse ways of explicating "God" is that, like the biblical picture of Jesus as the Christ, it ends up having two sorts of content—power and form.

These seem to be mutually exclusive. If the power mediated by religious symbols is the meaning of "God," and if theology's task is to state that meaning, then ontology does theology's job, and description of the patterns of relation between "God" and other symbols is irrelevant to theology. On the other hand, if theology's job is to explicate "God" and not to describe God, then its task is done by describing the patterns in which "God" is used and not by identifying "God" with the power of being. The passages that describe the patterns in which "God" is used and rely on warrants from analysis of revelations deal with the Christian doctrine of the Triune Godhead. Although it is not clear, the passages that rely on warrants from ontology and translate "God" into ontological categories seem to be dealing only with the First Person of the Trinity. If so, they must be understood in the context of the discussion of the distinctively Christian use of "God," i.e. in the context of the discussion of the Trinity. This is to say that the passages using warrants drawn from analysis of revelatory events exhibit Tillich's normative theological method and that the others, since they are inconsistent with the first group, violate his usual methodological practices. Thus, even the difficulties in Tillich's discussion of "God" both recapitulate a structural flaw we have repeatedly noted elsewhere in the system and support our analysis of the basis of this flaw.

8

THEOLOGY AND PROCLAMATION: AN APPRAISAL

We have taken seriously Paul Tillich's intention to think in accord with Scripture, to say what must be said today but "on the basis of the Apostles and Prophets." He proposes to identify the content of Scripture by subjecting biblical religious symbols, especially the biblical picture of Jesus as the Christ, to conceptualization, explanation, and criticism. This produces, not one overarching theological argument, but several related arguments in which biblical symbols, a philosophical account of religious experience, ontological analysis, historical research, and aesthetics are interwoven. Although we have examined how these various elements function as data, warrants, and backing in Tillich's arguments, we have not examined what sorts of proposals the conclusions to his arguments are. These arguments were entered as part of a program designed to aid Christian proclamation, to help the Church see what it must say today. Therefore, it will be useful to close this study of the fabric of Tillich's theology by considering the logical character of the conclusions of his arguments and how they are related to his published sermons. Just as an examination of Tillich's discussion of the symbol "God" served to draw together in review our proposals about the fabric of his thinking, so too, reflection on both his conclusions and his preaching may serve to focus our appraisal of his project.

The Content of Preaching

What sorts of proposals are made by the conclusions of Tillich's theological arguments, and how do they aid preaching? Two quite different answers may be given, depending on whether the content of biblical symbols such as "God" or "the picture of Jesus as the Christ" is said to be their form or the power mediated by them.

If the content of the symbols is their form, then the arguments developed in the course of conceptualizing and explaining the symbols support proposals of attitudes, policies for action, special ways of using certain concepts, and some beliefs. The sermons mostly urge on us these attitudes, exhort us to adopt these policies, and instruct us in these beliefs.

If the content of the symbols is the power of New Being, then the arguments developed in the course of criticizing the symbols support proposals about the basic features of religious experience and revelatory events. Such proposals are reflected, not in the content of the sermons, but in the strategy by which they are constructed.

By far, the greatest number of Tillich's published sermons urge us to adopt certain attitudes toward the world as a whole. We call them attitudes rather then beliefs or truth-claims because they do not admit of significant disagreement. Logically, they are rather like what R. M. Hare has called "bliks." They are all-pervasive attitudes, like that of the lunatic undergraduate who, in Hare's illustration, is certain that all dons are out to murder him. To the mildest don one might produce he will still reply, "Yes, but that was only his diabolical cunning; he's really plotting against me the whole time, like the rest of them."[1]

The attitudes Tillich commends are variations on a view that can be stated quite generally: although the world is shot through with estranging powers, precisely at the place in my personal life where they have their most destructive effects, there is mediated to me a healing, reconciling power. This attitude obviously has the same structure as the event of original Christian revelation as expressed in the form of the picture of Jesus as the Christ: The power of New Being (expressed by the symbol "resurrection") is present under the conditions of existence (expressed by the symbol "cross"). The pattern discovered in the biblical picture of Jesus as the Christ through conceptualization of the symbol, and found to characterize the way in which the miracle element of original revelation took place by explanation of the symbol, reappears in a homeletical mode as the characteristic form of the attitudes we are urged to adopt.

A classic instance of this occurs in the sermon, "You Are Accepted":

Grace strikes us when we are in great pain and restlessness. It strikes us when we walk through the dark valley of meaninglessness and empty life. It strikes us when we feel our separation is deeper then usual. . . . Sometimes at that moment a wave of light breaks into our darkness, and it is as though a voice were saying: "You are accepted. *You are accepted,* accepted by that which is

1. R. M. Hare, "Theology and Falsification," *New Essays in Philosophical Theology,* eds. Antony Flew and Alasdair MacIntyre (New York, Macmillan Co., 1955), p. 100.

greater than you, and the name of which you do not know. . . .
Simply accept the fact that you are accepted."[2]

Attitudes we are urged to adopt toward history,[3] nature,[4] and ourselves[5] all exhibit the same pattern. They are attitudes that construe actuality, "that which is real," as an ambiguous combination of the "existential" or disrupted and estranged dimensions of reality, and the "essential" or united and healing dimensions.

Tillich makes a second kind of proposal in his sermons when he urges us to adopt certain policies for action. These policies are variations on a theme too, for they all give a structure or shape to behavior that conforms to the structure of the basic Christian attitude to the world as a whole. In a sermon on the story of Jesus' anointment at the house of Simon the leper (Mark 14:3–9), Tillich points out that "the history of mankind is the history of men and women who wasted themselves and were not afraid of doing so." He then goes on to urge us: "Keep yourself open for the creative moment which may appear in the midst of what seemed to be waste."[6] In effect, we are told always to act so that the pattern of our actions conforms to the pattern of the distinctively Christian attitude. Be prepared to act in league with creative forces that are

2. Paul Tillich, *The Shaking of the Foundations* (New York, Charles Scribner's Sons, 1953), pp. 161–62.

3. E.g. *The Shaking of the Foundations*, p. 106; *The New Being*, pp. 57–58.

4. *The Shaking of the Foundations*, p. 85.

5. E.g. ibid., Chaps. 2 ("We Live in Two Orders"), 3 ("The Paradox of the Beatitudes"), 13 ("Knowledge Through Love"); Paul Tillich, *The Eternal Now* (New York, Charles Scribner's Sons, 1963), Chap. 7 ("Spiritual Presence").

6. *The New Being*, pp. 47–48.

present in the midst of what is destructive, even though your action may itself seem senseless and wasteful.

Tillich usually calls this policy of openness, not "love" as one might have expected from the New Testament, but "courage." To the attitude "Accept the fact that you are accepted" conforms the policy "Be courageous! Say Yes to yourself in spite of the anxiety of the No."[7] More concretely, this policy means, for example, that one would persist courageously in his honest religious doubts, despite their potentially destructive effects. The very courage exhibited in doing so is an expression in practice of an attitude that finds constructive forces, e.g. intellectual honesty and integrity, in the midst of what is destructive, e.g. wracking doubt and despair. To be sure, this courage is joyful and thankful and even loving, not stoically grim. Nevertheless, joy, thanks, and love are understood as modes of courage.[8] Whereas Braithwaite interprets Christian religious discourse as expressive of the policy decision to adopt an *agapeistic* mode of life, Tillich interprets much of it as an expression of the policy of being "courageous" in spite of all that threatens to make life meaningless.

When Tillich comes to the point in the sermon when he must stress specifically what has to be said *today* "on the basis of the Apostles and Prophets," he regularly proposes either an attitude or a policy. This is true, as we shall see, even though in the course of the sermon he makes other sorts of proposals too. It is clear that proposals of attitudes are more basic than proposals of policies,

7. *The Eternal Now*, pp. 152–53.
8. On "joy" and "courage" see *The Eternal Now*, p. 21, and *The New Being*, pp. 141–52; on "thanks" see *The Eternal Now*, pp. 173–83; on "love" see *The Shaking of the Foundations*, pp. 111–13.

however, since the policies are proposed only on the ground that they are the policies most appropriate to characteristic Christian attitudes.

In a few sermons Tillich makes a third kind of proposal when he argues that we believe certain truth-claims. Before we go further it is important to be clear about the difference between proposals of attitudes and proposals of beliefs. By a proposal of belief, we mean the proposal of a truth-claim. Here we follow William Christian's suggestion that there are four conditions in which we might take a religious proposal as a truth-claim.[9] First, it must be capable of self-consistent formulation. Second, it must be liable to significant disagreement. If it cannot be consistently negated, it seems to have no significant consequences and nothing could count for or against its being true. In that case, no significant truth-claim has been made. Third, the proposal must permit a reference to a logical subject. The term used for the logical subject must put others in mind of what is being talked about. In order to do this, it must be possible to give information about the logical subject of a proposal in addition to the information given in the proposal itself. More particularly, if someone is not put in mind of the logical subject of your proposal (e.g. "YHWH") by your initial reference to that subject (e.g. "YHWH revealed himself in Jesus Christ"), then it must be possible to adduce some fact or other as a starting point for your reference and to use some interpretive category by which to connect this fact with the logical subject. Furthermore, the fact must be independent of the proposal so that it is logically possible to accept the fact without accepting the proposal. Thus, in order to explain who YHWH is,

9. William Christian, *Meaning and Truth in Religion* (Princeton, Princeton University Press, 1964), pp. 24–34.

one might relate him to a fact (e.g. the ancient Hebrew's conquest of Palestine) by an interpretive category (e.g. "cause" or "controller of historical destiny") and say "YHWH is the one who caused the Canaanites to fall before the Israelite army." Fourth, the proposal must permit some support for the assignment of its predicate to its subject. That involves bringing up some fact as a datum in accord with some principle of judgment, or warrant, that permits one's move to the conclusion in which the logical predicate is assigned to the logical subject. The principle of judgment must be formulated "in the frame of" the relevant predicate. If we said "YHWH is the most Holy One," we could support the assignment of holy to YHWH by showing that in events of encounter with YHWH (the "facts") all the features noted by Otto in the experience of the holy (the "principles of judgment") are present in an eminent degree. If we said "Jesus is divine," we could support the assignment of the predicate to its subject by showing that in encounters with Jesus (the "facts") the healing power of being was mediated to us (a "principle of judgment" provided by Tillich's analysis of experiences of the "divine").

Tillich's proposal, "Accept the fact that you are accepted," appears to include a proposal for belief: "You are accepted." But the appearance is misleading. The conditions in which I would accept this proposal and affirm, "I am accepted," are not the conditions in which the proposal could be accepted as a truth-claim. For one thing, the proposal is not open to significant disagreement. The basis of the claim, "I am accepted," is not any kind of evidence that I have in fact been reunited with myself, others, and God. Rather, it is an attitude that excludes by definition the possibility of disconfirmation. Were I to protest, "No, I am not accepted, for there are many forces at work in my life alienating me from myself, others, and God," I would be told that I had misunderstood what was meant by acceptance. No amount of destructive forces in my life could count against the claim addressed to me, "You are accepted." "Accept the fact that you are accepted" is an exhortation to adopt an attitude, not an invitation to believe a truth. Furthermore, the proposal, "Accept the fact that you are accepted," does not permit reference to its logical subject. This may be seen if we change the proposal grammatically from the passive to the active voice: "X accepts you." Who or what is x? We are expressly told that we cannot know.

There are a few places in Tillich's sermons where he clearly is proposing beliefs. Some of these are historical. We are asked to believe that in his confession Peter "asserted that the decisive thing of history had appeared, and that the Christ, the bearer of the new, had come in this man Jesus."[10] We are told that, "in the picture of Jesus as the Christ, which appeared to him at the moment of his greatest separation from other men, from himself and God," Paul "found himself accepted in spite of his being rejected."[11] Several historical claims concern Jesus. "In the midst of the old creation there is a New Creation, and . . . this New Creation is manifest in Jesus who is called the Christ."[12] Indeed, "in Him this New Being is present in such a way that it determines his life. . . . The New Being that forms his life is not created by Him. He is created by it."[13] For precisely this reason, "The Christ had to suffer and die, because

10. *The Shaking of the Foundations,* pp. 143–44.
11. Ibid., p. 160.
12. *The New Being,* p. 18.
13. *The Shaking of the Foundations,* p. 101.

whenever the Divine appears in all its depth, It cannot be endured by men. It must be pushed away by the political powers, the religious authorities, and the bearers of cultural tradition."[14]

Historical truth-claims are never the burden of Tillich's sermons, however, and always when he does get to his point he shifts from proposing beliefs to proposing attitudes. It is characteristic, for instance, that after the claim regarding Paul noted above, Tillich does not move to the proposal that we too should believe that the picture of Jesus as the Christ mediates the "accepting" power of new being. Instead, he proposes, in effect, that we adopt toward the world as a whole the attitude that it is "accepting" of us.[15] Perhaps the most revealing instance of this occurs in a sermon on the question, "Has the Messiah Come?" The sermon begins with the claim that Christians, in contradistinction to Jews, believe that the Messiah has come. This is presented as a fact-claim about the Messiah. Furthermore, Tillich notes that one reason Jews give for rejecting the claim that the Messiah has come is that demonic forces are still too much in evidence in the world. But Tillich does not then urge that, nevertheless, we should believe that as a matter of fact the Messiah has come. Instead, he changes the character of the proposal. To say that the Messiah has come is to say that "Our eyes have seen His salvation." That is not to claim that something specifiable happened; rather, it is to adopt an attitude. It is to say that we should construe experience as including always and everywhere a mixture of saving or healing forces and estranging or destructive forces:[16]

14. Ibid., p. 147.
15. Cf. ibid., pp. 160–63; *The New Being,* pp. 112–13.
16. *The New Being,* pp. 93–96.

Salvation is a child and when it grows up it is crucified. Only he who can see power under weakness, the whole under the fragment, victory under defeat, glory under suffering, innocence under guilt, sanctity under sin, life under death can say: Mine eyes have seen thy salvation.[17]

Tillich proposes a few beliefs that are not historical. For example, we are asked to believe that "God does not leave the world at any place, in any time, without saviours—without healing power."[18] In another place we are told that "Something new has come, a new reality, a new being, a Spirit distinguished from our spirit yet able to make itself understood to our spirit, beyond us and yet in us."[19] As the contexts of these and all such proposals make clear, the claim that is made concerns men and things that go on in their lives. More particularly, it concerns what we have called "ontological disease" and "ontological healing." There can be no doubt that these proposals for belief do form part of the burden of the few sermons in which they appear. Even so, in the two sermons cited here as illustrations, there is a subtle shift from proposing beliefs to proposing attitudes. For example, after telling us that God never leaves us without saviours, and after identifying "salvation" with "conquest of enslaving powers," Tillich concludes to the proposal, not that we believe thus-and-such about our needs and how they may be met, but that we adopt toward life the attitude that in all our states liberating forces are at work.[20] Proposals of attitudes are over-

17. Ibid., p. 95.
18. *The Eternal Now*, p. 116.
19. *The Shaking of the Foundations*, p. 135.
20. *The Eternal Now*, p. 121.

whelmingly more important and more basic in Tillich's sermons than proposals of beliefs.

A fourth kind of proposal in Tillich's sermons concerns the meaning of major religious concepts. In the famous sermon, "You Are Accepted," which has already been cited several times, Tillich instructs us in the meaning of the terms "sin" and "grace":

> I should like to suggest another word to you, not as a substitute for the word "sin," but as a useful clue in the interpretation of the word "sin": "separation." . . . Perhaps the word "sin" has the same root as the word "asunder." In any case, *sin is separation*.[21]

> Grace is the *re*union of life with life, the *re*conciliation of the self with itself. Grace is the acceptance of that which is rejected.[22]

Other sermons explain such terms as "flesh,"[23] "love,"[24] "forgiveness,"[25] and "Messiah."[26]

In every case one could easily get the impression that Tillich was instructing the religiously ignorant in how Christians normally use key religious concepts. His procedure, however, shows that this is misleading. He regularly shows the "meaning" of a term by contrasting the way it is usually used, even by many Christians, with what he claims is its "real meaning." For instance, he tells us that

21. *The Shaking of the Foundations,* p. 154.
22. Ibid., p. 156.
23. Ibid., p. 133.
24. *The New Being,* p. 174.
25. Ibid., p. 10.
26. Ibid., p. 15.

"providence" "really means . . . the courage to accept life in the power of that which is more than life. Paul calls it the love of God."[27] A great many theologically sophisticated Christians would be quite astonished at this information, since they have not used "providence" that way at all. What Tillich presents as a descriptive proposal about how Christians use their central concepts turns out on closer inspection to be a prescriptive proposal about how they ought to use those concepts.

Even Tillich's proposals about the meaning of key concepts are subordinate to his proposals of attitudes. He regularly prescribes the "meaning" of major theological concepts by reference to some variation on the antithesis "existence/essence" or "estrangement/ reconciliation" or "brokenness/healing." When terms such as "flesh" or "sin" and "spirit" or "grace" are used in sermons in reference to man, they are used to express one aspect or the other of the experience of finding the healing power of new being in the midst of existential estrangement. But when they are used in relation to "life" or "history" or "the world" or "Jesus Christ" or "God," they are used to express one aspect or the other of the basic Christian attitude. Thus, even when Tillich begins sermons as a teacher instructing his congregation in the meaning of basic Christian concepts, he ends up making the main burden of his sermon an exhortation to adopt an attitude.

What is the relation between the four classes of proposals made in Tillich's sermons and the conclusions of his theological arguments? The relation seems straightforward enough. The conclusions of theological arguments state what the sermons propose, but with an important shift of emphasis. Tillich actually says what he

27. Ibid., pp. 57–58.

thinks needs to be said today "on the basis of the Apostles and Prophets" in his sermons. But the sermons do not arise directly out of what the Apostles and Prophets themselves said, i.e. out of Scripture. Rather they are based on biblical symbols only after they have been systematically conceptualized, explained, and criticized in theological arguments. The content of the sermons is derived directly from what theological reflection concludes ought to be said today, and only indirectly from the Apostles and Prophets on whom they are supposedly based. A large class of theological conclusions concerns the nature of saving and revelatory events, both past and present. This provides most of the proposals of belief made in the sermons. Since revelatory events involve one's coming to a sudden insight, these conclusions also provide the sermonic proposals of attitudes. For the insight that comes with ontological healing becomes the Christian's most basic attitude toward the world, and it is this attitude that many of the sermons urge us to adopt. Historical judgments constitute a small number of theological conclusions and provide the historical fact-claims proposed in some of Tillich's sermons.

There is a notable shift in emphasis as one moves to the sermons from the theology. Tillich stresses in his analysis of saving and revelatory events that the power of being is necessarily always mediated through particular finite symbols and that of these Jesus as the Christ is the final and normative one. For that reason he devotes a great deal of space to a discussion both of Jesus as the Christ and of the biblical picture of Jesus as the Christ. These discussions concluded to important fact-claims about the way in which Jesus and the picture may function in revelatory events today. The sermons, however, only rarely urge us to believe these claims. Indeed, they almost never present the biblical picture of Jesus as the Christ so that someone might receive it ecstatically. Moreover, while they do exhort us to adopt attitudes exhibiting the "cruciform" pattern of the basic Christian attitude, they rarely relate that attitude to the biblical picture of Jesus as the Christ and the function that the picture could play in our lives as mediator of the power of new being.

The Strategy of Preaching

There is quite a different relation between the conclusions of Tillich's theological arguments and his sermons when the content of the symbols is said to be the power they mediate. We have seen that when the content of symbols is said to be this power, then the chief function of theology is not so much to explicate the symbols as to describe the dynamics of revelatory events. The analysis of revelatory events shows that on their receiving side they are marked by an experience of the holy and by a new insight.

Sermons provide at least the objective possibility for the occurrence of dependent revelatory events today when they present aspects of the biblical picture of Jesus as the Christ. There is no way to guarantee that a revelatory event will in fact occur, since there is no way to control experiences of the holy. But it is possible, by the way the sermon is structured, to help elicit insight. That is, a sermon may bring the hearer to share the perspective or attitude of the preacher, not so much because of its persuasive argument as because of its structure. More specifically, it is possible to structure Christian sermons so that they elicit insight into the presence of the reconciling power of new being precisely in the midst of estrangement.

The structure of many of Tillich's sermons functions in just this way. There is a characteristic pattern. First, they draw attention to one way or another in which we currently experience our existential state of estrangement and disruption, and they boldly face the meaninglessness it gives to our lives. That expresses what Tillich takes to be the usual perspective or attitude of his hearers toward their lives. Then he draws attention to the passion with which we protest that state of affairs in the name of an overriding concern for wholeness. By holding together before his hearer both his existential predicament and his passionate concern about that state of affairs, Tillich tries to elicit a new insight, a new perspective or attitude on life as a whole: The world is not simply characterized by existential estrangement; in addition, there is present to me a grasp of eternally valid standards of the good, the true, and the beautiful or I should not have had any basis for my protest or the courage to be concerned in an ultimate way.

This pattern is present, for example, in "The Shaking of the Foundations."[28] First, Tillich notes widespread disillusionment with man's capacity to rule himself and his world. It is an awareness of our predicament. Man has unlimited creative capacities, but "when he rests complacently on his cultural creativity or on his technical progress, on his political institutions or on his religious systems, he has been thrown into disintegration and chaos." Then Tillich shifts perspective: "There is scarcely one thing about which we may not be cynical. But we *cannot* be cynical about the shaking of the foundations of everything! I have never encountered anyone who seriously was cynical about that." The fact that we protest "the shaking of the foundations" must be held together with the fact that the foundations do shake. Holding them together may bring us to share the

28. *The Shaking of the Foundations,* pp. 2–11.

perspective of the prophets who saw "that they belonged within two spheres, the changeable *and* the unchangeable." A great many of Tillich's sermons exhibit variations on this pattern.[29]

The structure we are discussing is not necessarily identical with the formal organization of a sermon. "The Eternal Now,"[30] for example, is formally organized into three parts, the first reflecting on anxieties evoked by the future, the second on the curses inflicted on us by the past, and the third on the way the present is at once a fleeting moment and an abiding reality. But in its strategy this sermon follows the structure we have outlined. The first two points draw attention to a way in which we experience our existential predicament: Both the uncertainties of the future and the shackles of the past make what we do in the present seem meaningless. And the present seems to be no more than "the ever-moving boundary line between past and future." But then in the midst of his third point Tillich switches perspective. He points out that it is also the case that from another point of view all we ever experience directly is the present, which we experience constantly. We think of ourselves as having a present; we think of the future and the past as ours. In short, we affirm our lives in time; "we accept the present and do not care that it is gone in the moment we accept it. We live in it and it is renewed for us in every new 'present.' " The fact that we do have the courage to accept the present and act in it must be held together with the fact that temporal change raises questions about the worth of what we do. Holding them together may elicit

29. E.g. *The Shaking of the Foundations,* Chaps. 2 ("We Live in Two Orders"), 3 ("The Paradox of the Beatitudes"), 5 ("Meditation: The Mystery of Time").
30. *The Eternal Now,* pp. 122–32.

the insight in which we are "aware of this 'eternal now' in the temporal 'now.' "

Furthermore, this strategy may be used several times in the same sermon to elicit a sequence of insights each of which approaches more closely the insight to which Tillich is most concerned to bring the hearer. In "The Depth of Existence,"[31] he is concerned to get the hearer to share the perspective in which it is both natural to quest for the "depth dimension" of life as a whole and to recognize that it is found only through suffering. Tillich goes through the pattern of shifting perspectives in relation to three familiar modes of inquiry in order to elicit the insight that the question of "depth" arises in a partial way in each of them, and always in connection with a form of suffering. Study of the physical world always involves going "deeper" than received opinions and theories, but it also involves a sense of wonder "that there is something and not nothing," which arises in the context of anxieties created by our common finitude and contingency. Reflection on ourselves involves questions about goals and motives for our actions, where we constantly press to get below the superficial, but it also involves radical questions about the meaning of life as a whole, asked from a different perspective created by personal tragedy. Investigation of our common communal life involves a quest for ever deeper analyses of social ills and the means for healing them. It also involves a different order of question concerning the very possibility of hope for social improvement and raised by the most apocalyptic of historical calamities. Tillich points out that in each case the radical "depth" question, coming out of some sort of suffering, might by itself simply lead

31. *The Shaking of the Foundations*, pp. 52–63.

to despair. But in each case he switches perspective by showing that the very concern manifested in asking the question is itself an expression of a continuing apprehension of the "deepest" ground of meaning precisely in the midst of the very estrangement from evident meaning that causes the suffering.

It is appropriate that sermons whose main burden is to urge the adoption of an attitude should by their very structure elicit the insight that puts a man into that attitude. It is not necessary to claim that Tillich deliberately used theological judgments as rules guiding the shaping of sermons. For our purposes it is enough to point out that, regardless of the psychology of authorship, the sermons Tillich wrote manifest in their strategy the conclusions to which he comes in theological argument about the dynamics of revelatory events.

Furthermore, it is appropriate that the attitudes urged by these sermons and the insights they elicit concern, not the biblical picture of Jesus as the Christ, but human experience in general. For the theological conclusions manifested in these sermons arise in connection with the judgment that the content of Scripture is not the picture in its particularity, but the power mediated by the picture and also by an indefinite number of other particular, concrete entities. Even when these sermons do present aspects of the picture, they do so only to move from the particular to the general, urging an attitude toward life as a whole rather than toward Jesus as the Christ. The only irony is that a set of theological arguments that could not show any connection between the formal properties of the picture of Jesus as the Christ and the fact that it does mediate the power of new being does, nevertheless, provide guidelines for giving a form to sermons based on that picture that enables them to elicit the insight allegedly elicited by the picture!

Critique

What is the logical status of the most important conclusions for which Tillich enters theological arguments in his *Systematic Theology?* If theological arguments are developed as an aid and guide to Christian proclamation, then the preaching aided and guided by these arguments ought to be a reliable index to where the weight of importance lies in the arguments. On that basis we have shown excellent ground for the claim that the most important conclusions of Tillich's theological arguments are proposals of attitudes and descriptions of revelatory events. These are not the only sorts of proposals for which Tillich argues. His theological conclusions also include proposals of beliefs, of policies for action, and of correct word usage. But so far as aid to preaching is concerned, it is clear from the way that they give shape and content to sermons that descriptions of revelatory events and proposals of attitudes toward the world are the most important sorts of conclusions.

If this judgment is correct, it reveals a curious inconsistency in Tillich's theological program. We noted at the outset that for Tillich the basic purpose of theology is to explicate the content of the biblical picture of Jesus as the Christ and of all other biblical symbols insofar as they are related to the picture. In short, the central task of theology is, in Tillich's sense of the word, "christological." This suggests that the important conclusions for which arguments would be entered would concern the picture and related symbols and what they uniquely have to say. In fact, however, the important conclusions do not make proposals about Jesus as the Christ or about the biblical picture or about any particular religious symbol. Instead, they are highly general and are "based" on the biblical picture only in the sense that the picture "suggests" an attitude one might adopt toward life as a whole and provides an instance of a revelatory event from which one may safely generalize about all revelatory events. They are christological proposals only in the sense that they propose that we "see" the same cruciform pattern that was present in the Christ event as the pattern of occurrences taking place everywhere and at all times.

Here is a decisive place at which to test the success of Tillich's method of engaging in theological reflection that is at once fair to historical–critical problems and yet "in accord with Scripture." Any criticism at this point is necessarily criticism of Tillich's Christology. In contrast to Tillich, one striking characteristic of New Testament proclamation, despite all of its inner diversity, is that it does make truth-claims. To be sure, it also proposes policies for action and the adoption of an attitude toward life as a whole that "sees" life already drawn into the eschatological era, already covenanted with by God, already redeemed. But fundamental to both of these is a proposal of belief, viz., that this state of affairs, and consequently the appropriateness of the policies for action, is contingent on the particular fact of Jesus Christ's life, ministry, death, and resurrection. The major question that must be put to Tillich's entire theological enterprise is whether, by shifting the center of importance in his theology from the proposal of belief to a proposal of attitude, he throws Christian proclamation shaped by his theology seriously out of line with New Testament proclamation.[32] If that happens, can it be claimed that this is a theological

32. On this point there is a convergence of critical judgment given from a Barthian Protestant perspective on the one side (cf. McKelway, *The Systematic*

method which allows us to say today what must be said on the basis of the Apostles and Prophets?

It is not difficult to identify the element in Tillich's theological method that produces this distortion in his conclusions. We have seen that the crucial move in his procedure is the decision to construe Scripture on an aesthetic model. Scripture is "authority" for theology only insofar as it is understood as a verbal icon, a "picture." In this lies the value of his method, because it seems to promise a way of maintaining the importance of Scripture for theology even after historical-critical study has revealed the errors in its facts and the cultural parochialism of its world-view and ethics.

But precisely the same move creates the difficulties we have noted. If Scripture is to be interpreted on the model of a picture, then, like any important aesthetic object, it must be understood not to make any claims. The content of a work of art is simply the work itself. It does not inform us of anything. At most it may elicit a new insight so that thereafter we "look" at the world differently. Thus, it may cause us to adopt a new attitude, draw us into a new perspective on "the way things are." But a picture certainly cannot be said to include as part of its content any claim that the world ought to be looked at that way because the work of art somehow made things to be "that way." If works of art provide the basic model on which Scripture is to be understood, then it is inevitable that theological conclusions drawn "in accord with Scripture" will reverse the biblical order and stress attitudes over beliefs. Whatever difficulties there may be with Tillich's *Systematic Theology*

Theology of Paul Tillich, pp. 179–82), and from a Roman Catholic perspective on the other (cf. Tavard, *Paul Tillich and the Christian Message,* passim).

as a critical statement of the Christian community's confession of faith, they do not arise from the fact that he makes use of ontological analysis or philosophical description of religious experience, or too little use of historical findings. It may be that his theological method requires him to use these things in unfortunate ways. However, it is far from clear that any theologian can avoid using them in *some* way, and Tillich at least has the virtue of developing these elements in a clearly labeled way. Instead, the difficulties with his theology seem to grow out of the very thing that makes his one of the boldest and most suggestive theological proposals of the modern period, the doctrine of *analogia imaginis*.

INDEX

91, 102; norm of, 5–8; sources for, 2–3; structure of, 13–17, 176; subject matter of, 3, 25, 34. *See also* Theological arguments, Theological statements, Warrants for theological arguments

Toulmin, Stephen, 9, 12, 13

Trinity: component symbols of, 168; essential Trinity, 83; God qua creator, 169–70; and revelation in Christ, 167–68; trinitarian principles, 16, 154–55, 161–64, 166–67

Ultimate concern, 22, 28–29, 31, 85
Unconditioned power of being, 28, 44, 79; and being-itself, 59; and ontological analysis, 58–59

Verbal icon, 105, 107, 110, 111, 112, 139

Warrants for theological arguments, 11; and aesthetics, 147–52; and analysis of revelatory occurrences, 19–20, 23, 25, 31, 49, 86; and ontology, 51–52, 62, 77–80; and use of religious symbols, 24–25, 165

Whistler, James McNeill, 151
Wimsatt, W. K., 109